Practical Guide
To Brood
Mares

Practical Guide To Brood Mares

Alfred Goulder

SWAN·HILL
PRESS

Copyright © 1995 by Alfred Goulder (Text)
Copyright © 1995 by Sally Partington
(Illustrations except pages 32, 33, 43, 125 (top))

First published in the UK in 1995
by Swan Hill Press
an imprint of Airlife Publishing Ltd

British Library Cataloguing in Publication Data
  A catalogue record for this book
  is available from the British Library

ISBN 1 85310 480 9

Typeset by Hewer Text Composition Services, Edinburgh
Printed by Biddles Ltd, Guildford and King's Lynn.

Swan Hill Press
an imprint of Airlife Publishing Ltd
101 Longden Road, Shrewsbury SY3 9EB

Dedication

This book is dedicated to the young and future owners of brood mares of every type, with the hope that any knowledge gained from it will help to give these superb animals a better existence, and that they in return will give satisfaction and pleasure to the above enthusiast.

It is also dedicated to the memory of the late Duke of Norfolk and to his widow Lavinia, Duchess of Norfolk, for whom I worked for thirty-six years.

Dedication

Contents

Contents

Foreword

Peter Willett

I have known Alf Goulder for more than twenty-five years and was both very pleased and proud when he invited me to contribute a Foreword to his book. His skills, experience and dedication to his profession make him exceptionally well qualified to impart his knowledge to everyone ready to pay attention to his advice.

As stud-groom to the 16th Duke of Norfolk, and later to his widow Lavinia, Duchess of Norfolk, at Angmering Park Stud, Alf has been responsible for the welfare of some of the best horses of the last quarter of a century up to the time they went into training. They included Ragstone, winner of the Ascot Gold Cup, Moon Madness, winner of the St Leger, and Sheriff's Star, winner of the Coronation Cup. Those are races in the top echelon of the British Turf, and horses capable of winning them can be brought to maturity only if they have been given the best possible start in life.

Visitors to Angmering Park have always been impressed by Alf's combination of a sympathetic but firm, no nonsense approach to mares and young bloodstock. Proper mental education is as important as the physical development of young bloodstock if their potential as racehorses is to be realised, and Alf Goulder's command of the full range of a stud-groom's responsibilities made him one of a select few in his profession.

These qualities are difficult, if not impossible, to convey in the pages of a book. Possession of them adds immensely to the authority of Alf Goulder's opinions and counsel, and I recommend his book unreservedly to all those engaged, or who wish to become engaged, in the care of Thoroughbreds.

Introduction

Michael Ashton, MC, MRCVS

Having known and worked with Alfred Goulder for more than thirty years, I find it is both a privilege and pleasure to write these words. This is a practical book written by a knowledgeable and experienced stud-groom from his own observations of what is a highly technical subject. The book is well laid out, not difficult to understand and is very readable.

Acknowledgements

I am extremely grateful to Her Grace Lavinia, Duchess of Norfolk, LG, CBE, for all her help and kindness; also veterinary consultant Michael Ashton, MC, MRCVS, who gave me so much encouragement and read the final draft and corrected it. Many thanks to Katherine Lewis who typed the manuscript, read and corrected my English and helped me with so much enthusiasm during the preparation of this book. I should also like to thank Sally Partington for all her hard work with both the text and the line drawings. The generous support from Clive Horwood and his input into how I should prepare the book and photographs is much appreciated. Many thanks to Michael Bowley and Jayne Arbon, who worked with me on the stud, for all their help; and to Lindsey Goulder.

The illustrations are reproduced by permission of the following, together with my grateful thanks:

Her Grace Lavinia, Duchess of Norfolk, LG, CBE.
Veterinary Consultant, B.W. Eagles, BSc, B.Vet.Med, MRCVS.
Veterinary Surgeon, R.G. Allpress, BVSc, MRCVS.
Miss B. Swire.
Peter Button.
Philip Goulder.
Sally Partington.

The author and publishers are grateful to the following for permission to quote copyright material in the book:

Living Water by Olaf Alexandersson. Turnstone Press Ltd, Wellingborough, Northamptonshire.
The Veterinary Record, 23 August 1980. Article taken from Grassland Management for Horses. Animal Health Trust, Balaton Lodge, Newmarket, Suffolk.
The Thoroughbred Breeder, December 1990. Part article taken from Veterinary Aspects of Stud Layout and Design. Animal Health Trust, Balaton Lodge, Newmarket, Suffolk.
Animal Management 1923. Prepared by the Veterinary Department of the War Office, Imperial House, Kingsway, London WC2.
Weatherbys and The National Light Horse Breeding Society.

Preface

During the forty-six years I have spent working with horses hardly a day has passed without my learning something different about these marvellous creatures. Obviously my knowledge has been gained for the most part in the world of Thoroughbreds, but I have always believed regardless of breed or type that the same principles of horse management apply. So I have tried to explain these principles as clearly and concisely as possible so that every brood mare owner will have a reliable guide to follow.

Whatever your motivation for breeding a horse or pony you must be prepared for expense, disappointments and frustrations, but if you weather all these the end result will make it worthwhile. In short the breeder must be an optimist with boundless amounts of patience. All youngstock must be given the time to finish growing and to strengthen. You cannot make a two-year-old into a three-year-old!

Finally, well-trained stable and stud staff, male or female, are invaluable. The very nature of the work means that they must be willing to work long hours with dedication, in all kinds of weather, day or night, for the animal's well-being. They must also be even-tempered at all times, even when provoked by a bite or a kick from a yearling.

Sadly the importance of their work is not always fully recognised, but without their knowledge, patience and ability no youngster will go on to achieve its full potential.

Alf Goulder

1
Paddocks and Pasture Maintenance

The ideal for any stud farm is to have paddocks with old swards for pasture, and if these are not available every effort must be made to create a similar environment. Old swards are meadows or paddocks which have been seeded down for ten or fifteen years or more, regularly maintained by chain harrowing and rolling, and rested from horses by alternating sheep and cattle on the grazing.

Old swards contain a superb variety of meadow grasses such as timothy, cocksfoot, sweet vernal, fescues – both the sheep and meadow kind – foxtail, lamb's tail and crested dog's tail; not to mention a host of other sweet grasses. These are all very nutritious, palatable and, most importantly, prolific growers. The other huge advantage of old swards is that over the course of many years these grasses establish such a good root formation. The density of this strong base, which is spongy underfoot, helps to eliminate any unnecessary jarring to the developing limbs of foals and yearlings, whether walking or galloping. This is especially pertinent after the succession of dry summers we have enjoyed or endured, when the incidence of splints and bony enlargements suffered by youngstock has increased markedly.

Nowadays the majority of paddocks are seeded down with a selection of the above grasses but are dominated by rye grass and clover. Red clover is not a fast-growing plant, but white clover can cover a lot of ground if not kept under control. Too high a concentration of white clover is undesirable because of its high nitrogen content, which can lead to kidney problems in youngstock, and can also upset their calcium balance.

Grass will grow on most types of soil, but it must be appreciated that the type of grazing which will fatten bullocks or lambs is not the best grazing for horses or ponies. Foals and yearlings do not need to be fat, but to grow good bone and muscle. Older horses, whether riding horses, hunters, racehorses, ponies or breeding stock, should never be over-fat, as this will inevitably lead to complications such as laminitis.

Weeds should always be kept under control. Badly neglected swards, where fifty per cent or more of the grass cover is composed of weeds, should be ploughed up and resown.

The job of paddock maintenance is a never-ending one, from spring until autumn, year in and year out; but without it grazing horses will ruin even the best of swards.

Harrowing and rolling are the first two chores to be considered. The principal reason for harrowing is to open up the surface of the soil to enable the air and the frost to penetrate. Harrowing also removes the accumulation of dead grasses and levels off the divots and poached areas of mud which are always found around gateways. Uneven and cut-up paddocks, when the ground is either very dry or frozen hard, can have a disastrous effect on young joints and limbs. Undoubtedly the process of harrowing will bring flints and stones to the surface, and these should be picked up whenever possible to avoid unnecessary injuries.

Chain harrows should be used in late autumn and again in early spring. The optimum tractor speed for this job is 7mph (11km per hour), which enables the harrows to draw more evenly and smoothly over the ground and therefore produces a much better finish to the lay. Cross-harrowing is even more beneficial, as it aerates the soil still further.

Rolling is normally carried out about a fortnight after harrowing. The Cambridge roller, with its corrugated surface, is the most effective for this job, as it does not compress the soil into too hard a surface, which could be further worsened by dry weather, but allows the air to circulate freely into the soil. If rolling is carried out at about 5mph (8km per hour) all the uneven surfaces will be correctly put down and the time and effort involved will be well rewarded.

Having completed the harrowing and rolling it is important not to overlook the condition of the soil, which can deteriorate tremendously if neglected. Nitrogen, phosphorus and calcium are taken from the soil when horses are grazing. These elements, as well as some others, are also washed deeper into the soil by the rain and may therefore not be readily available to the plants growing on the surface.

On any land that is intended for horses it is vital to check on a regular basis, by means of a detailed soil analysis, that in spite of the demands on these elements there remains an adequate mineral supply for continued vigorous growth. In many downland areas, for example, paddocks may have a predominantly chalk base, but the soil at the depth where root formation occurs might be found to have a low pH value (i.e. a high level of acidity). In this case an application of lime, at the recommended amount per acre, would redress the balance.

Strictly speaking, lime is calcium oxide. Calcium is almost invariably present in the soil in sufficient quantity for the requirements of plants. However, calcium oxide, calcium hydroxide and calcium carbonate are added as soil sweeteners and to liberate other chemicals in the soil as well as improving the texture of heavy ground. All forms of lime, including chalk, are identical for these purposes, except that some act more rapidly and others have better moisture-holding qualities. Once the lime content in the soil has been brought up to the required level, experience has shown that an application of basic slag every fourth year thereafter will be sufficient to top up the lime content and keep the paddocks in good condition.

Basic slag is vitrified cinder, a slow-acting phosphatic fertiliser which also supplies lime. It is a by-product of the steel industry and has to be ground by machinery; the coarser the grinding, the slower the action. Slag can remain in the soil for many years, but its quality varies and analysis may show anything from eight per cent to eighteen per cent phosphoric acid content. The solubility and consequently the availability of the phosphoric acid also varies. This is quoted on the basis of solubility in citric acid. If the slag is over eighty per cent soluble it is of good quality and if it is under forty per cent soluble it is poor quality and therefore exceptionally slow-acting. Depending on the quality, between 5 and 7cwt (254 and 355kg) of basic slag per acre is a sufficient quantity for most paddocks. If basic slag is not easily available in your area, change to an alternative source of phosphate; but it is always worth having the soil analysed to check whether or not an application of phosphate is necessary.

In addition to lime and basic slag, concentrated organic seaweed produced in liquid form is another beneficial dressing for any paddock. The best time of year for the annual spraying is mid-May and a ratio of one gallon (4.5 litres) of seaweed solution to nine gallons (40.5 litres) of water should be used. Seaweed is a valuable substitute for dung as it is much richer in potash. It is almost completely lacking in phosphates, but nevertheless will still balance with lime and slag to produce the much-needed trace elements which living organisms require, albeit in minute quantities, for normal growth.

The mineral requirements of the horse, including trace elements, are given in Chapter 3. But if horses do not seem to thrive, have the soil checked to establish whether a mineral deficiency may be the reason. If analysis shows that the soil is indeed lacking in one or other of the essential minerals, a mineral mixture, which will include all the trace elements the horse requires, can be fed to cover all possible deficiencies. Mineral mixtures can be obtained from merchants specialising in horse feeds.

The topping of paddocks in early summer is very important, particularly when the weather is warm and humid. In these weather conditions grass grows very rapidly and it will soon run to seed. The way to prevent this happening is to top the grass when it is in flower to about 6in (15cm) high. This will stop the strength of the grass growth being wasted on seed production and will encourage a stronger root formation as well as a fresh growth of younger foliage, which is far more palatable for young stock.

Early summer is also the time when unwanted weeds such as nettles, docks, thistles, brambles, gorse and buttercups grow. If these weeds are not dug up or treated in some way they will eventually take over the paddock. It is so much better to walk the paddocks and spot-spray them than to spray with a tractor and spraying unit. Spot-spraying with a selective weed-killer in a hand spray container when the weeds are about 3 to 4in (8 to 10cm) high stops both reseeding and any further spreading of root formations. It is also less costly than tractor spraying and prevents any inadvertent slowing of grass growth or, worse still, killing off of nutritious plants such as clover, dandelions or trefoil. The paddock should be rested for the recommended amount of time after spraying and this period varies according to the product used.

Special attention should be paid to weeds or other plants

in the paddock area which can be actively poisonous or otherwise dangerous to stock. Ragwort, a tall, yellow flowering plant, should be pulled up before it goes to seed or root development takes place. Seed can be carried by the wind over large areas, and landowners are under legal obligation to dispose of this poisonous weed. Ragwort should be pulled up by hand and burnt if possible. If it is thrown down and left to dry out, it then becomes more poisonous to both cattle and horses and, if eaten, will cause liver damage. Bracken should also be treated in this way, but in this case regular applications of lime should ensure that the soil is not suitable for its growth.

Other poisonous weeds or plants which should be avoided at all costs include yew, deadly nightshade, foxglove, hemlock, aconite, white bryony, water dropwort, mares tails and dodder. Among trees and shrubs, not only the well-known yew but also laurel, privet, laburnum and rhododendrons are poisonous to horses. Caution should be taken with oak trees as even these can be dangerous, especially when there has been a heavy fall of acorns, since acorns, though safe enough in small amounts, can be harmful if eaten in large quantities.

Apple and pear trees should also not be encouraged as horses love the fruit and too much of it could result in severe colic or even cause a horse to choke to death. In any case of colic the vet should be called, especially if you suspect that any of the weeds or shrubs listed above may be responsible. Even if you know that your paddocks are clear of any poisonous plants, check the possibility that they may have been reached through the fence. Tell the vet immediately what you think the horse might have eaten.

Horse droppings should be picked up daily in all paddocks, as this is the only way to avoid severe worm infestation. All horses carry a percentage of worms and worm larvae in the intestine, which are then passed out in the faeces on to the pasture. The horses eat the contaminated grass and the cycle is completed with sometimes fatal results, unless strict controls are observed.

On the arrival of any new horse to the stud or stables, a sample of the faeces should be taken to your nearest veterinary practice and a worm count should be taken. This will give an accurate evaluation of the percentage of worms present in every gram of faeces and the horse or pony can be treated with the appropriate drug. Redworm, round-worm, tapeworm and bots can cause considerable damage to the gut and blood vessel walls, as well as causing colic, poor condition and diarrhoea. It cannot be stressed often enough how important worm control is for maintaining a healthy animal. There are a range of excellent drugs avail-able nowadays which are very easy to administer in the form of a paste. The horse should be wormed every five to six weeks, especially through the danger months between March and September. It is also advisable to alternate the type of drug used each time the horse is due to be wormed as this will avoid any danger of the animal forming an immunity to one particular drug.

Another form of worm control is to move cattle on to a paddock when the horses are moved out, as the cattle will eat the remaining grass together with the worm residue. When the time comes to move the cattle out, sheep can end the rotation as they will eat the grasses much shorter, and finally the paddock can be rested for three months. How-ever, this method is only practical for those with ready access to other stock.

It is essential that every paddock should have some form of windbreak. One of the most satisfactory is a beech hedge, which maintains its old leaves throughout the winter and if maintained to a height of 8ft (2.5m) with a width of 18ft

23

Water
hemlock
or
water
dropwort.
The
flowers
of
hemlock
are
very
similar.

Foxglove.

The
dark
blue
flowers
of
aconite
or
monkshood.

Ragwort.

Deadly nightshade: its berries are a glossy purplish-black.

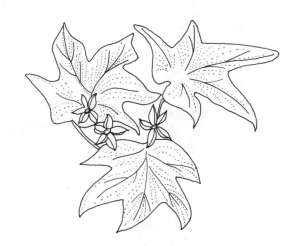

*White bryony.
Both white and black bryony are poisonous to horses, although they are not in fact related to each other. Both plants, however, have small white flowers and reddish-orange berries.*

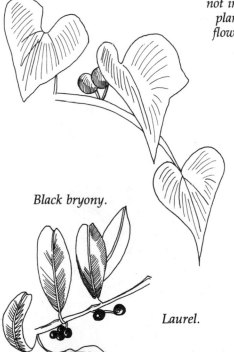

Black bryony.

Laurel.

Mares tail or horsetail.

25

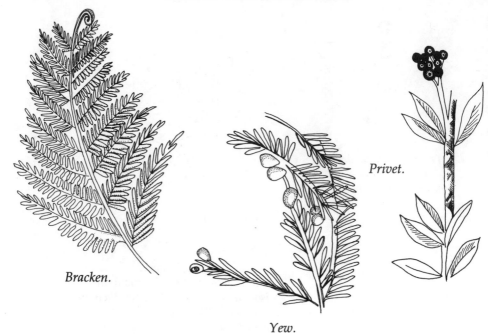

Bracken.

Privet.

Yew.

Box is not dissimilar to privet and can also be poisonous to horses. It is best avoided.

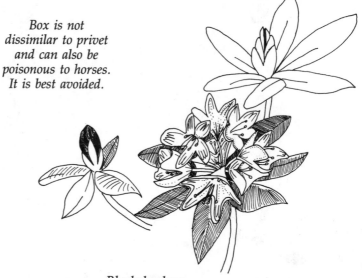

Rhododendron.

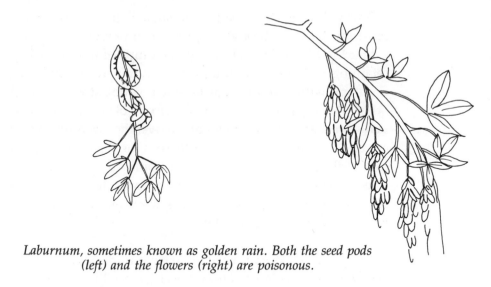

Laburnum, sometimes known as golden rain. Both the seed pods (left) and the flowers (right) are poisonous.

Horse chestnut

Oak

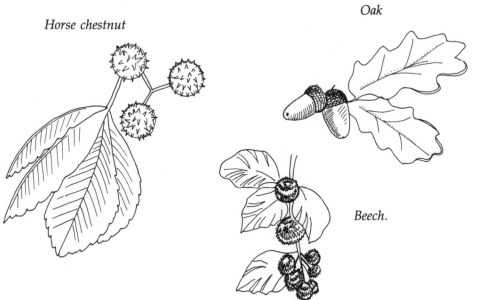

Beech.

Even these familiar trees can be dangerous to horses. Acorns, beech nuts and, more rarely, conkers can all cause problems if eaten in large quantities.

27

(5.5m) will provide considerable shelter. It must be fenced off from the stock though to prevent to prevent them from eating their way through it! Small clumps of trees or a high retaining wall also provide protection, but walls can cause problems with potential injuries when young stock race each other. Field shelters are another mixed blessing, as horses very rarely seem to use them in wet weather, and when they are used in the summer to escape from the flies, young stock can easily kick one another in the confined space. If either trees or hedges are used, care must be taken to see that there are no poisonous trees or bushes such as yew, privet or laurel within reach of the horses.

Fencing paddocks is a very expensive undertaking. Whatever kind of fencing is chosen accidents will undoubtedly

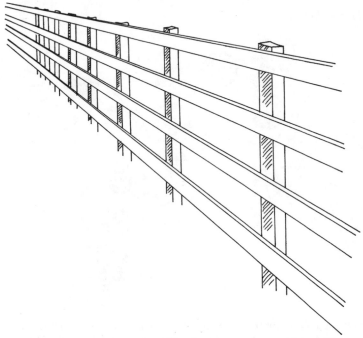

Fencing
Good stout oak post-and-rails provides the most durable fencing.

happen, but most stud and horse owners seem to favour wooden post and rails. These certainly seem preferable to any form of wire, which is not to be recommended, even if it is coated in plastic. Barbed wire and permanent sheep netting should be avoided at all costs.

Ideally oak post and rails are the most durable, but also the most expensive, so a cheaper soft wood such as fir is perfectly acceptable so long as it is well seasoned and treated with a preservative. It is easier for access purposes if five-bar gates are at least 10ft (3m) wide, and if the paddocks have rounded corners this will help to prevent unnecessary accidents, as all horses have a habit of running into the corners. If the rails are painted white it does give the youngsters a chance to see them better. Often young stock will not gallop so much if turned out in a hill field and this can have additional benefits in that the continual walking up and down hill will help to strengthen their quarters and develop their shoulders. Obviously the quieter the location of the paddocks the less likely youngsters will be to get upset and gallop, so try to avoid siting them next to roads or railways or public rights of way.

If a natural fresh water supply is not available in the paddocks the next best thing is to use self-feeding water troughs. Nothing is worse than buckets and baths filled with water in the corner of a paddock as they will cause accidents sooner or later if foals and yearlings are turned out together. It is much more prudent to have self-feeding troughs conveniently placed to one side of the paddock and to encase them in wooden boards to prevent the corners protruding and so avoid the possibility of injury. Heating appliance manufacturers have produced a trough heating element which stops the water freezing in the winter months; the disadvantage of this useful device is that it requires an electrical supply to run it. It is also worth having stop-cocks fitted to any troughs in paddocks, and troughs should be cleaned out periodically to stop bacteria and slime from spreading.

Most mare owners will have to manage with whatever land they have available to them, but in an ideal world a small private stud with an average of sixteen animals would need to be of at least a hundred acres, divided into at least ten paddocks. The following table gives an example of how to use a hundred acres most effectively.

7 mares with foals, two paddocks of ten acres each	20
3 mares without foals, one paddock of ten acres	10
4 yearling colts, two paddocks of ten acres each	20
2 yearling fillies, one paddock of ten acres	10
4 resting paddocks for rotation of ten acres each	40
	Total: 100

Provision should also be made for an isolation paddock for mares and foals returning to or arriving from other studs and stables or from abroad. This will also give an opportunity to worm the new arrivals whilst in the paddock, which will help cut down the worm infestation before they are eventually turned out with other horses a week to ten days after their arrival. In addition it is a good idea to have a very small area of grass with boarded sides for use as a nursery paddock. This will be most useful when turning mares with new foals out for the first time.

2

Stabling

The first consideration when building a new stable block is the selection of a good site. This should be a large flat area with protection from the prevailing winds, and it should be in close proximity to the surrounding paddocks and pasture land in order to help save time when leading the horses to and from the paddocks. There must be a reliable source of water and also facilities for a drainage system, or at least enough room to install one.

Before any building can be designed a decision must be made about whether to have rows of boxes, in which case they can all be south-facing, or whether to have the boxes built around a central courtyard. It is also worth considering whether to build a separate yearling yard. Separate yards are beneficial as foals and yearlings will not have built up resistance to viruses such as coughs and colds, which are highly infectious. In any case there will have to be at least one separate yard for weanlings, and some provision will have to be made for an isolation block for new arrivals and to help prevent the spread of disease in the event of an outbreak.

American-style barns are in use all over the world and are becoming increasingly popular in this country. However, in my own opinion they have certain disadvantages which mean that they are not really suitable for use on stud farms. In this day and age, when horses are travelling worldwide, the risk of infection from contagious diseases is greater than ever, and to my mind the style of living conditions in American barns can encourage the easy transmission of disease to other horses, no matter how well managed the barns are.

The following description is of the ideal loose box design. Generally speaking, the best materials also tend to be the most expensive, and in many cases different materials can be used to help cut costs. However, bear in mind that cheaper alternatives may well have hidden drawbacks.

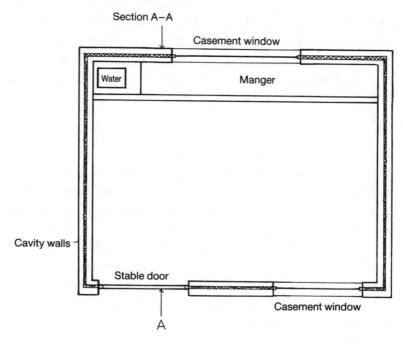

PLAN VIEW OF STABLE

Walls should be made of brick or block and should be of double thickness – in other words of cavity wall construction – so that insulating materials can be inserted in between. The foundations should have a damp course up to just above ground level and the ground area of each box should be 16ft by 12ft (5m by 3.7m) to accommodate a mare with foal at foot. The walls should be at least 12ft (3.7m) high, before a sloping rather than a flat roof is added.

Ideally the roof should be tiled or slated, but this is a costly process. Roofing felt is much cheaper, and has proved to be quite adequate. Air vents should be set into the ridge of each stable roof, at least two vents per box. Skylights let into the roof are also a good idea as they allow direct entry of sunlight into the boxes. It is a fact that sunlight does actively help to

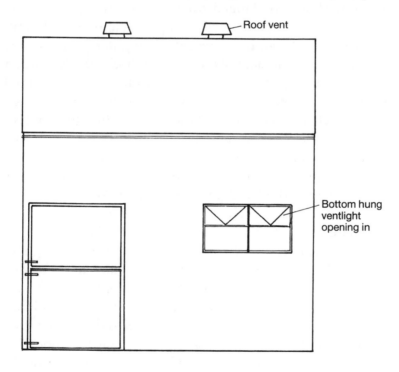

Roof vent

Bottom hung ventlight opening in

FRONT ELEVATION OF STABLE

keep certain kinds of bacteria and parasites at bay; and in general good ventilation and light, clean conditions are not tolerated by most disease-producing bacteria and viruses.

Many yards have a roof overhang along the front of the line of boxes. This is mainly for the convenience of the staff as it helps keep them dry in bad weather, but it has the disadvantage of keeping valuable sunlight off the boxes as well. This is another criticism which can also be levelled at American-style barns, which tend not to allow the entry of as much sunlight as does the traditional loose box.

Long stable windows let in plenty of light, which is useful if the top stable door is shut up for some reason. The window should be hinged from the lower edge or centre, so that it can be opened with an upward and inward slant. The direction taken by a current of air entering a stable is determined by the slant of the window, and with this design the air will be thrown upwards well over the animal standing underneath. The advantage of this is that the air will be well diffused before it reaches the animal and the risk of a draught is avoided. The object of ventilation is to change the air of a building or box frequently enough to keep it fresh without allowing a draught to touch the occupants. This is especially important in stables designed for foals, as foals are so susceptible to draughts at such a young age.

Windows can be placed anywhere in the box, as long as the horse cannot reach them to break them. The more light in the box the better; but it is always a good idea to make sure that the windows have bars on the inside for protection, and laminated safety glass should always be used to minimise breakages. The best possible site for a hinged window such as that described above is on the wall opposite the door. This will enable the air to circulate fully and be carried straight through, thus ensuring the most beneficial ventilation.

Stable doors should be 5ft (1.5m) wide and should open outwards. The wider door will allow plenty of room for the mare and foal entering or leaving the box, without any danger of them knocking their hip joints. These joints, if injured, take a considerable amount of time to heal and they look very unsightly. Vertical roller bars fitted to the left and right of the door frames are a great help, especially if the horse is highly strung or excited. Roller bars are cylinders made of hard wood, approximately 10in (25.4cm) in circumference and 2ft 8in (.8m) high, which can be fixed to the door frame about 1ft 8in (.5m) above the floor. A spindle goes

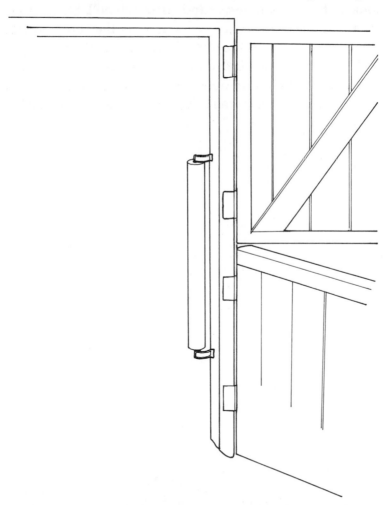

Vertical roller bars fixed to the door frame of the loose box will help prevent injury to the hip joints of mare and foal.

down through the bar so that it revolves when brushed against. If the horse does hit the side of the door frame the roller will revolve with the movement and the horse will not be hurt.

The doorway should be at least 8ft (2.5m) high. Unfortunately even at this height it is still possible for a startled horse to throw its head up and strike the poll. Stable doors are a permanent means of ventilation, as they are normally fitted with half doors, the top half left open and hooked back so that the horse can look out. Sliding bolts should be fitted to both top and bottom doors. Some horses learn the knack of undoing bolts, and if the bolt is recessed and fitted flush to

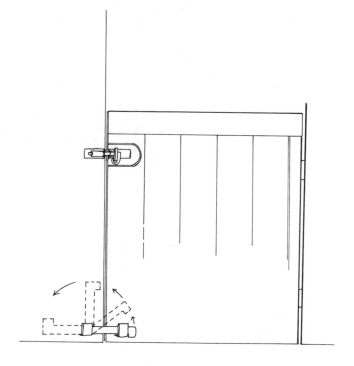

Kick-over bolts fitted to the bottom of stable doors will ensure that the door stays shut even if the upper bolt should somehow come undone. A top bolt fitted flush to the door will make it much harder for the horse itself to catch hold of and undo.

the door it is much harder for the horse to undo it when playing with it. The bottom doors should also be fitted with kick-over bolts to prevent the horse getting out in the event of his undoing the top one. Great care should be taken when selecting the door bolts that there are no sharp edges for the horse to cut himself on and no protruding bolts for the horse's headcollar to get caught on.

The top edge of the bottom door is normally covered with tin to prevent the horse chewing the wood. Unfortunately tin will show signs of wear after a time, especially if the occupant of the box is a crib-biter or windsucker. The horse will grip the door with its teeth in order to suck in air. There will be indentations in the tin from the teeth marks, and eventually the constant wear will cause the tin to split and become ragged, which will be not only unsightly but potentially dangerous to the horse.

Stainless steel strips can be used in place of tin as these are much more durable, and if drilled and screwed on to the door will not look out of place. Care must be taken to keep the strips flush with the door to avoid injury to the horse. Have them cut to the correct length for the top edge of the bottom door, with an overlap either side for fixing round each end to give a smooth finish all along the top. Suitable strips can be made by a blacksmith or a builders' merchant. Finally, ensure that the bottom half of the door is high enough to prevent the horse from jumping out. Around 4ft 8in (1.4m) is usually high enough to deter most horses.

Having chosen the format for the stable yard and watched its construction, attention must be turned to the smaller details and other necessary buildings. The box floors are normally laid down with cement or concrete with a slope of not more than 2in (5cm) in every 10ft (3m) for drainage purposes. However, concrete has two drawbacks. The first is that it conducts heat, so that when a foal is lying down it will suffer heat loss unless the box is deeply bedded, and the second is that it can be slippery underfoot. Chalk floors, on the other hand, are not slippery, are porous and retain heat.

For a chalk floor to be any good it must be laid down to a thickness of 2ft 6in to 3ft (.7m to .9m) and then heavily rolled with a vibrator roller. Otherwise the chalk will tend to sink and urine may start to lie in pools. Chalk floors also need to be regularly maintained. There will be a certain amount of wear to the chalk over a period of time, for example where the horse stands, in the door area, around the manger and in the centre of the box. When the floor becomes uneven, two or three inches of chalk can be scraped off the surface. Fine chalk is replaced and then heavily rolled. This should be done at least once a year or, if the floor is showing a lot of wear, earlier. An ideal time for resurfacing would be when the boxes are being steam cleaned. The top layer of chalk should also be stripped and relaid in the same way after any contagious infection.

Mangers should run the width of the back wall of the box. The main reason for this is so that the feed can be scattered along it, enabling the foal to feed on its own, away from the mare. This is especially important if the brood mare is greedy. The rim of the manger should be wide enough to prevent it being gripped by teeth and so avoid providing the perfect crib-biting site. The manger itself should be broad and have well-rounded corners. There should be no protruding objects in the box such as sharp corners, nails or hay racks.

Hay should be fed loose. It is never advisable to use hay nets with young stock because of the dangers. Hay nets need to be tied up high so that there is no danger of a horse getting its feet entangled in one. With mares and foals it will obviously be difficult to find a safe height because of the size difference of mare and foal. Low enough for the foal to reach will not be high enough to be safe for the mare. In addition a net which is tied at a safe height when it is filled full will sag and hang lower when it is emptied overnight. And even if you think a net is tied at a safe height it is possible for a foal to rear up in order to reach it more easily and entangle its front feet this way with disastrous consequences. Horse owners who are not used to foals may not appreciate just how dangerous a hay net can be in these circumstances. Much better to shake hay up in a clean corner. If you know your animals and muck out regularly you will know which corner will be best. Horses are grazing animals and eating from a clean corner is more natural for them.

A tie ring should be let into the wall of each box at a suitable height and position and the walls should be rendered smooth. This facilitates steam-cleaning them when it is necessary. If the walls are painted white it does help to give a lighter, airier feel to the box, which will usually need to be painted annually.

Water can be supplied to the boxes in automatic drinking troughs set into one end of the manger. These are obviously very labour-saving, but they must be regularly checked for cleanliness. Certain horses like to drink as they are eating their feed; some food does escape from their mouths and sinks to the bottom of the drinker, and if this is not cleaned out it will turn the water sour. After the animal has finished its meal, the water should be changed. The only other problem when using automatic drinkers is that they make it harder to find out how much water a particular animal is drinking.

It is possible to fit heated wrap-around tape to the inlet pipes to stop the water freezing in winter. This consists of a flexible wire element which is wrapped around the pipe and works on a thermostat from its own transformer. The pipe and element are covered with plastic foam, and from the down pipe to the drinker the pipe is protected with a secure plastic outer cover.

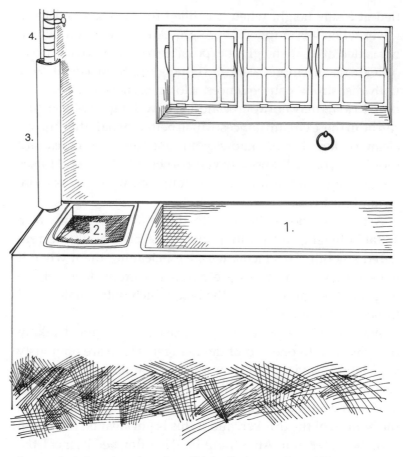

Loose box interior showing (1) built-in manger, (2) automatic drinker, with inlet pipe protected by (3) plastic casing and heated by (4) special wrap-around tape.

Every box should have an electric light fitting but this must be well out of the horse's reach. Switches are normally placed outside each box, where they will need to be properly insulated against weather conditions. It is also important that they are well out of the reach of playful young stock. If the horse can reach the switch when it is looking over the door it will more than likely start to fiddle with it and may well pull it off the wall.

It is very helpful to have good powerful outside lights for the whole yard to make winter work easier. Some thought must be given to the surface of the path directly outside the boxes and to the surface of the yard as a whole. Remember that the yard will be swept daily, so some form of concrete or tarmacadam will be easier to maintain. The ideal path is tarred with a non-slip proofed surface on top of which is laid fine gravel, which should be raked. Concrete with herring-bone grooving is also useful for both anti-slip and drainage purposes, and in case of ice and snow agricultural salt or sand will give a better grip.

The feed room should be situated so that there is not too much unnecessary walking during feeding. It should be a dry, well-ventilated room and the grain bins should be checked and cleaned regularly to prevent grain mites. The grain mite or weevil is a long-snouted beetle which thrives on grain. Grain stored in a damp barn or shed which is not regularly cleaned out provides ideal conditions for weevils and soon the place will be infested with them. Ideally oats should be bought in small quantities and used up so that bins can be checked and cleaned before fresh oats are put in.

Power points will also be needed in the feed room for the hot water boiler which is used to cook linseed for the mashes. Next to the feed room there should be a small store for the yard implements and for first aid equipment, and this room should be fitted with a sink with both hot and cold water. Any cleaning of headcollars or foal slips can be done here.

A foaling box should be situated so that a member of staff can keep watch easily, especially at night, without too much disturbance to the mare. The box should be free from draughts and there should be some provision for heating lamps (infra-red lamps) in the event of a sickly or weak foal being born or if the weather is particularly bad for an early foaling. The large stallion studs are very well-equipped for the many mares that foal down during the season and these studs have a sitting-up room for the staff next to the foaling box, so that the mare can be observed without the staff having to go outside. Obviously there must be a telephone at hand in case of emergencies.

If stallion boxes are needed they should be placed well away from the main stable block. The same also applies to storage space for hay and straw: these buildings should always be a little apart from the main yard as a fire precaution. Storage barns must be clean, dry and rain-proof. A small leak in the roof can spoil a considerable amount of hay or straw in a very short time. Hay and straw should not be stacked too close to each other as there is always a risk of spontaneous combustion, especially if the hay overheats.

Fire extinguishers should be within easy reach of both barns and stables and the staff should be taught how to use them. A fire officer from any fire station will advise you as to which type of extinguisher is most suitable for your needs.

Any horse lorry on the premises should be kept covered if possible, but not in the barns with the hay and straw. The loading and unloading of young stock can be difficult, and so to minimise the risk of accidents it is helpful to have a loading ramp. This prevents the youngsters from slipping off the lorry ramp and because they are fenced in it is much easier to persuade them to load at the first time of asking.

A loading ramp can be built as follows. The base of the ramp should be made from breeze-blocks, built in an oblong 9ft (2.7m) wide, 17ft (5m) long and 2ft 6in (.7m) high. The area inside the oblong is then filled in with soil and grassed over. Wooden panels 8ft (2.5m) high are then erected along the sides and back, leaving a 5ft (1.5m) opening on one side. At this opening there should be a gently graded slope down to ground level which should also have boarded sides. The completed ramp is L-shaped. The horse can walk up the grass ramp and then turn to face into the lorry, which is much safer than trying to coax youngsters up the lorry ramp with no sides to guide them.

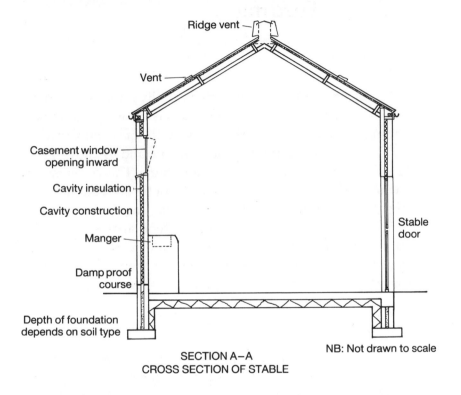

SECTION A–A
CROSS SECTION OF STABLE

3

Feeding

The correct feeding of every horse is vitally important and it must be remembered that each horse has its own individual requirements. It is therefore necessary to know how much food to give in the form of grain and hay, and to know how these are converted into flesh, fat and bone. This conversion is what is known as nutrition and it can be divided into six constituents: protein, carbohydrate or energy, minerals, vitamins, water and fibrous material. Food analysis enables one to ascertain the exact percentage of a particular constituent in any foodstuff, so that one can then calculate the exact nutritional value of any diet.

Proteins

Proteins are a flesh-making nutrient group and are essential for the development of the body. A higher percentage of proteins is needed for lactation, for in-foal mares, for foals and for yearlings. Without them a youngster's growth will be severely restricted or at worst it could die. On the other hand, if proteins are fed in excess of the body's requirements for any length of time they can have all manner of adverse effects. These can range from liver disorders to swollen legs, laminitis, diarrhoea, over-heating and over-production of fat. Obesity in mares can be the cause of difficulties with conception and can also lead to problems at foaling.

Proteins consist of amino acids, which are available from

oats, beans, linseed and alfalfa. Lysine is a very high quality amino acid which can be found in soya beans and lupin seed. This particularly high quality protein is needed to promote foetal development and aid lactation. A dietary intake of these amino acids is essential as horses are unable to produce them naturally within the body by any other means.

Carbohydrates

The function of carbohydrates is to produce fat, energy and heat. Energy is essential for every bodily process. The raw material which provides this energy can be either digestible fibre from plant materials, simple plant sugars, cereal starches or fats and oils of animal or vegetable origin. Underfeeding carbohydrates will affect the growth rate of youngsters and the milk supply in mares, as well as the overall condition of the animals. However, high levels of plant sugars and cereal starch have been associated with digestive disorders and laminitis. Finally, fats, starches and sugars are worthless as energy producers without the presence of proteins.

Minerals

Most of the skeleton of the horse is made from minerals, which are derived from grasses in the pasture. These minerals are vital to the horse and this is why pasture management must be carried out so assiduously. The following table shows the mineral requirements of the horse:

Bone Flour	40	parts
Calcium Carbonate, Limestone or Chalk	35	"
Common Salt	15	"
Flower of Sulphur	5	"

Magnesium Sulphate	2	"
Iron Sulphate	1	"
Sodium Sulphate	1	"
Trace Element Mixture	1	"
(Copper, Cobalt, Manganese and Iodine)		
	100 Parts	

The presence of calcium and salts in the food is essential, especially in young stock. The salts in the body are not only found in the bones, but in the blood, hair, horn, muscle and sweat. They direct the constant changes taking place in the body, and when they are excreted they must be replaced.

These essential minerals, when taken up by the plant, undergo changes which make them more readily available to the animal than when they are in the form of chemical salts in the soil. They are important for normal growth of bone and development.

Vitamins

Vitamins are required by the horse to enable the complex chemical reactions vital for life to take place.

Vitamin A is supplied by cod liver oil and green foodstuffs.

Vitamin B is found in yeast and bran.

Vitamin C can be stored in the liver.

Vitamin D is needed to guard against rickets.

Vitamin E is used for muscular movement.

The circumstances in which horses are kept affect their vitamin requirements. Although the body is able to store some vitamins, prolonged stabling does necessitate vitamin supplementation, as most conventional hay and cereal diets are deficient in them. Grazing horses generally need no added vitamins, unless a particular area is geologically found to be lacking in certain minerals or vitamins, as in granite-based areas of the country where the soil cover tends to be poor.

Water

Water forms a considerable portion of all foods, even those which are considered to be dry. The amount of water in grain varies from ten to twelve per cent and can be as high as ninety per cent in roots. Drinking water must be available at all times and it should be clean and pure. Unfortunately the underground water supply is sometimes contaminated by seepage of material waste, such as chemical and artificial manures. This means that most people rely on their local water authority for their water supply. Their water will be clean but it will also contain added chlorine. Although chlorine is said not to affect the horse, some authorities consider that the presence of chlorine in the water can hinder the body's performance by one per cent. That is, the horse may win ninety-nine races out of a hundred, but not the hundredth. This may seem a very small amount, but when trying to breed performance horses every factor must be considered.

Therefore, while natural untreated water should be preferred, all water on a stud or stable should be analysed, especially if it is from a private supply such as a bore hole, spring or stream. The water analysis will reveal whether the supply is clean enough and it will also show the different minerals present in the water. Lastly, special care should be taken as to the siting of any water storage tanks that are needed. It is best to situate them under ground level, where the water will be kept much cooler in hot weather conditions and the growth of bacteria or algae in the water will be discouraged.

The following extract is taken from *Living Water* by Olaf Alexandersson. The book is about the life and work of the

Austrian naturalist and inventor, Viktor Schauberger. Schauberger held extreme views, but his thoughts on water are worth considering.

> Water which sinks into the earth from the atmosphere will pick up salts and minerals and other substances which restore its vitality; it is enlivened by isolation from light and air. But there is also a certain journey in both time and distance that the water must make underground before it becomes internally mature. Water is mature if the air it has absorbed contains at least ninety-six per cent carbon content of which there is a proportion of solid matter. From this inner maturity the quality and the internal strength of the water depend . . .

> Schauberger did not approve of pumped subsurface water as drinking water. This water forced artificially from the depths was 'immature' – it had not yet passed through the whole of its natural cycle, and therefore in the long term would be injurious to man, animals and even plants. Only the water that runs out from the soil by itself in the form of springs and streams is suitable as drinking water.

Unfortunately few of us are lucky enough to be able to rely on springs and streams for our water supplies nowadays.

Fibrous Material

Fibrous material in the form of chop or chaff, sugar beet, oats, barley, maize and other digestible fibre is very important for the stabled horse, as it provides the bulk in the feed. Bulk prevents the bolting of feeds and helps to maintain a healthy digestive system. Herbivorous animals graze continuously in their natural state, and bulk serves to lengthen the feeding time of the stabled horse, so that the natural eating pattern is copied more closely. Fibre must be supplied to prevent extended periods when the horse is without feed as this can upset the delicate digestive balance.

The Horse's Digestive System

Without going into too much detail it is important to understand what happens to the food from the time it enters the horse's mouth until the remaining undigested material is excreted as droppings. This will help explain the relative digestibility of the foodstuff and show how the nutrients are extracted from it.

The digestive tract of the horse can be divided into five areas: the mouth, the stomach, the small intestine, the caecum and the colon.

The food is broken up in the *mouth* by the molar teeth and saturated with saliva. It is then passed to the back of the mouth in the shape of a ball. A horse can use up to ten gallons (thirty-five litres) of saliva during a twenty-four-

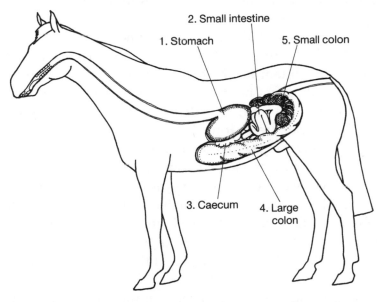

The small intestine alone is approximately 25 metres long and, as can be seen above, is packed into a relatively small area and frequently bent back on itself. It is here that most of the blockages of which colic is a symptom occur.

hour period. The saliva converts starch into sugar. The bulk in the diet which was discussed earlier is very important at this stage as it encourages slow mastication and a good flow of saliva, so that the digestive processes are started in the mouth. Slow mastication also helps to prevent choking.

The *stomach* of the horse is small and only half of the lining membrane secretes gastric juice. The exit from the stomach is larger than the entrance. The food is broken down further here, especially the flesh-forming elements.

In the *small intestine* the food is reduced to a liquid mass from which some of the nutrients are absorbed through the intestine walls. The intestinal juices convert starch into sugar, as do the pancreatic juices. Bile from the liver emulsifies fats and disinfects the bowel as well as breaking down the flesh-forming elements for absorption. The harmless bacteria always present in the digestive tract also aid the digestive processes at this stage.

The nutrients in the food are further absorbed in the *caecum*. These are by now in liquid form. The storing of liquid is important for the body's needs and to aid proper digestion. It cannot be stressed too often how vital it is for the horse's well-being that there is always an adequate supply of clean, fresh drinking water available.

The final part of the digestive tract consists of the *large and small colon*. Any remaining nutrient matter is absorbed before the waste is excreted. The waste is usually composed of the fibrous material, which has helped to ensure the thorough digestion of the feed. Judicious feeding keeps the bowels active and open, which prevents any absorption of waste matter into the system and thereby avoids disease.

The digestibility of food depends on the following factors. The quantity of food is important. It is better to feed little and often, as the horse is unable to vomit. The food quality must be good. A sample should be clean and free from dust. The

amount of feed should be tailored to the individual requirements of each horse. Food in excess of the animal's needs
causes diarrhoea or can ferment in the bowel and produce
toxins which are then absorbed into the system and affect the
animal's general health.

The horse's teeth can directly influence the ability to digest
feed. They should be checked at least annually and rasped
by your veterinary surgeon or a bona fide horse dentist. This
is a very specialised job and a cursory rasp up and down
without the proper equipment will not achieve anything and
will only waste your money. Few people realise how far
back in the horse's mouth the last molar is set, and it can only
be correctly rasped when a gag is fitted to the animal's
mouth in order to hold it open and stop the horse from biting
on the rasp. Irregular wear on the tables of the molars can
hinder mastication or at worst prevent it entirely on one side
of the mouth. This in turn prevents the feed from being
properly digested, so that the horse does not extract the full
value from its feed. Not only does this upset the balance of
the carefully planned diet, but it can endanger the horse, as
well as being an obvious waste of money as undigested
material will be excreted unnecessarily.

Feedstuffs

When adopting a new diet it is imperative to consider its
feeding value, the correct balance of food to aid digestion
and the quantity of food required by each animal.

The following is a brief explanation of the individual uses
of the various foodstuffs mentioned earlier in this chapter:
oats, barley, maize, bran, beans, linseed and hay.

Oats are the best and easiest grain to feed to horses
because they do not upset the digestive system unless fed
to excess. The protein level in oats should be well over nine
per cent and the highest quality oats are Canadian, Austra-

lian, Scottish and some English. Good oats should be plump, short, dust-free, of a good colour, dry and hard to touch. They should rattle when dropped on a hard surface. They should not smell and when bitten should taste like oatmeal. When buying oats in bulk it is a good idea to mix one or two of the aforementioned varieties.

Oats are essential for growing stock, but the quantity your particular animals require will depend on their breed and their purpose. One must remember with riding horses that they are fed according to the work they do and their rider's capabilities. If a horse becomes difficult to handle it is best to take it off oats and feed horse nuts which are available for all types of breeds and which contain the necessary nutritional requirements.

Barley is good horse food. It can be crushed and mixed with oats or boiled for several hours and then fed in a mash form. It is especially helpful for putting on flesh when a horse has lost condition, and it also has a high protein content.

Maize, on the other hand, while it is a very good conditioning food, has a poor protein content, so that it is not really suitable for young stock. It also only has a small percentage of mineral salts and these can equally easily be supplied in the form of mineral licks. Every animal should have access to a mineral lick.

Bran today is not as good as it used to be, as it contains less flour than in the past. Its feeding value lies merely in its laxative effect and for making mashes. It must be remembered that the calcium/phosphorus ratio of bran is completely incorrect, and extra calcium, in the form of limestone flour, must be provided when it is fed.

Beans are very nutritious. Their seeds carry a high protein level and contain a large proportion of flesh-forming elements. They are very easy to feed when ground, but should only be fed in small quantities as they can overheat the body if fed to excess. Nutritionists suggest that if beans are to be fed, soya bean meal is the best and cheapest which is commonly available.

Linseed is a good foodstuff for putting on weight, putting a gloss on the coat and also for use as a laxative. It is a small brown seed with a very tough husk which cannot be fed to horses in its natural form. The seeds would pass straight through the horse's body unchanged and if uncooked are completely indigestible. It is very important to soak the seed for at least twelve hours in water and then cook it for a minimum of four hours, preferably longer. Linseed boilers large or small can be bought for this purpose. They have a removable inside container to take the soaked linseed; this inner container is then surrounded by water which is kept simmering for up to eight hours. If it is not cooked properly, linseed can be toxic.

When it is thoroughly cooked it becomes a jelly-like substance which should be fed in small quantities. Linseed should be cooked fresh daily, approximately one average tea-cup per horse: if too large a quantity is given it could cause the animal to purge. The cooked linseed should be well mixed into the oats or other feed and is usually fed as an extra in the winter months.

Honey is a very useful additive when trying to encourage a fussy youngster to feed. It also helps to settle any dust that there may be in the feed.

There are of course compound feeds which can be fed in the form of pellets or nuts. There are many different types available to cater for the various categories of animal such as in-foal mares, weanlings or yearlings. These should provide a balanced diet, but if you feed nuts do remember that all horses are individuals and may sometimes have special requirements.

There are several different types of hay available but the main ones are as follows:

Meadow hay is grown on permanent grass land and can be distinguished by the large varieties of grasses it contains, the fineness of growth and by its superior aroma.

Seed hay is sown as a rotation crop for two or three years and is normally known as seed mixture. It is characterised by the small number of different grasses it contains, the vigour of their growth and its general hardness as compared with meadow hay. Seed hay contains a large proportion of rye grass and clover.

Lucerne hay grows with great luxuriance on soils where it flourishes and is cultivated especially for horses. It is known as Alfalfa and is a far superior source of protein.

Chaff or *Chop* is made from good quality seed hay and is cut into 1in (2.5cm) lengths with a chaff cutter. Chaff ensures the thorough mastication of the grain when mixed with it. It can also be bought with added molasses, but this is not always advisable as the molasses can cover up dusty poor quality hay or even straw.

All hay should be of a good colour, i.e. greenish or brownish but not yellow. It should be free from dust, crisp to feel, sweet to taste and have a pleasant aroma. The quality and character of hay is naturally affected by the soil on which it is produced. Some people prefer to buy their hay from areas that are known to produce good hay rather than make their own.

4

Conformation

In a brood mare conformation is just as important as, if not more important than, fashionable blood lines or even racing or jumping ability. Ideally, when looking for a potential brood mare, one should follow these guidelines on conformation.

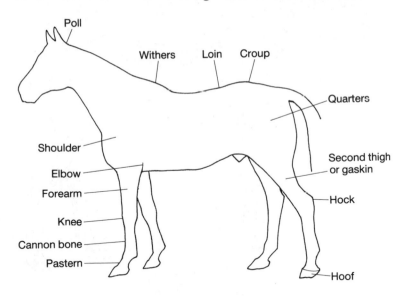

Points of the horse.

The Head

Looking at the mare sideways on, the head should not be too large in relation to her overall size. Obviously the perfect size and shape of head will vary from one breed to another. The Arab, for instance, has a very distinctive head; small and well-shaped, with its characteristic dished face. However, whether you are breeding Thoroughbreds, Arabs, show animals such as hunters, showjumpers or competition horses, the same basic principles apply, and a head which is out of proportion to the rest of the body is never a desirable trait. The bigger and heavier the head, the thicker the neck to support it, and this weight, especially when combined with the additional weight of a rider in the

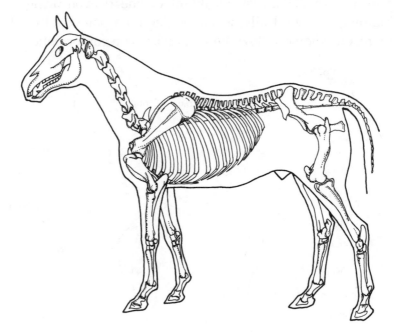

Skeleton of the horse.

forward seat, all puts extra strain on the front legs. For the racehorse or event horse, or any horse in a field of competition where speed is important, this can only be a disadvantage. It must be remembered that the horse's fore-legs support more than half of its body weight.

The distinctive Arab head.

There should be a good width between the eyes, which should be large and open with a kind expression, not too prominent, and set nicely, not too close together but well out on the side of the head. Small narrow eyes can often mean an ungenerous horse. Ears are normally upright and active, although actual size is only a matter of personal preference. Some people believe that large ears indicate a kind and generous nature.

Large and well-opened nostrils are desirable to facilitate breathing and the mouth must be correctly formed. Any

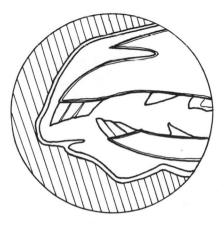

Parrot mouth is a hereditary defect in which the lower jaw is shorter than the upper and the incisors are unable to meet. It does not necessarily affect the horse's performance but in severe cases may mean he is unable to graze.

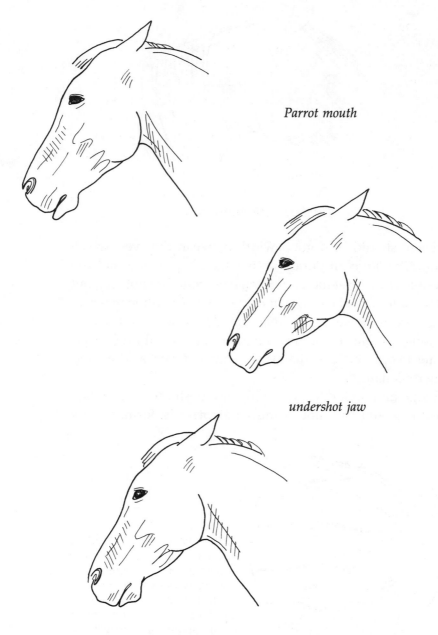

Parrot mouth

undershot jaw

normal jaw.

tendency towards a parrot mouth, where the upper jaw is too long for the lower, or the reverse, an undershot jaw, should be avoided, as both of these can affect a horse's ability to chew and digest food efficiently. A good depth through the jaw demonstrates good masticating power which in turn will benefit the digestion and subsequent condition. There should be enough room to put one's fist between the branches of the jaw: a good width here indicates that the horse has the capacity for easy breathing.

Some horses have a face which is convex from the forehead and tapers increasingly to the nostrils. This type of head is known as 'Roman nosed'. Others have a 'dished face' which follows a concave line from forehead to nostrils and is generally an indication of Arab influence. Unless the particular breed standard specifies otherwise, perhaps this latter type has the better-looking head.

Roman nosed.   *Dish faced.*

The Neck

The angle at which the head meets the neck is one of the most important features of conformation. If the neck is too thick at this point there will always be a problem with proper flexion of the neck, which in show animals or riding stock is vital. When the horse's head is in the correct position it is much easier for the rider to maintain control, and no amount of training or schooling will achieve this if the horse's basic conformation prevents it.

'The angle at which the head meets the neck is one of the most important features of conformation . . .'

The neck should be of proportionate length to both head and body, but not too heavy or bulky. Whatever the length it must be strong and muscular and set well on the wither to give a good natural carriage.

'When the horse's head is in the correct position (shown here) it is much easier for the rider to maintain control . . .' A head which is badly set on a too-thick neck will make this position difficult or impossible to achieve.

The Withers

A good wither should be able to take a saddle comfortably behind it so that the saddle does not move. Too high a wither is difficult to fit with saddlery and can cause rubbing and discomfort to the horse. A flat wither is equally difficult because a saddle will tend to slip forward or round.

The Back

The back should be short coupled, which is to say the distance from the withers to the croup should not be disproportionately long. There should be no sign of weakness such as a horse dipping its back when pressure is put on

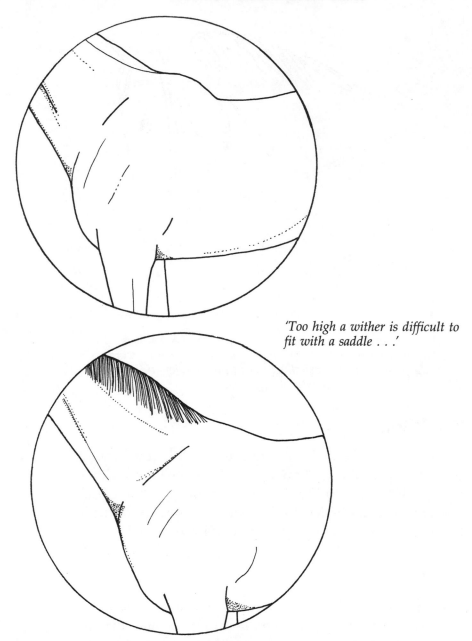

'Too high a wither is difficult to fit with a saddle . . .'

'A flat wither is equally difficult because a saddle will tend to slip forward . . .'

it. A long back can mean weakness, and it is often difficult to keep condition on a long-backed horse when in work. However, a length of back in a brood mare is not always a bad thing as it does allow more room for the mare to carry the growing foetus.

An unusually long back is often a weak back. Mares, however, tend to have slightly longer backs than stallions or geldings, to allow room to carry a foal.

The Barrel

The barrel of the mare gets its shape from the arch and depth of the ribs and the length of the back and loins. The ribs should be well rounded and deep so as to give plenty of room for the heart, lungs, stomach and bowels and they should reach well back so that there is not much space between the last rib and the point of the hip. A good deep barrel is what is meant by the old saying 'plenty of heart room', but in fact it allows the lungs more room to expand under stress such as the exertion of very fast work.

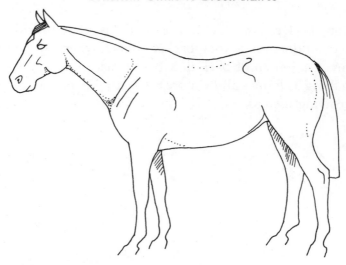

This horse is heavy-topped: its body appears large for its legs, and a horse of this type is often prone to leg problems.

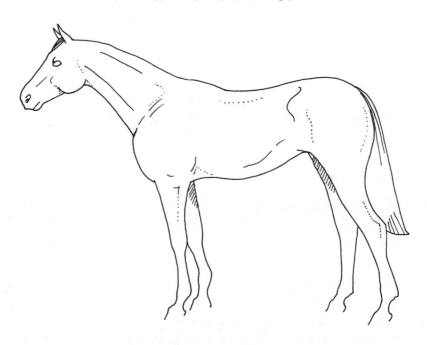

This horse is the opposite – over-tall and 'on the leg'.

Paddock and Pasture Management. (*Above*) Harrowing to open
up the surface of the soil to enable air and frost to penetrate.
(*Below*) Rolling with a Cambridge roller.

A beech hedge (*above*) or a circular clump of trees (*below*) make good windbreaks.

Ascarids or white worm.

Tape worm.

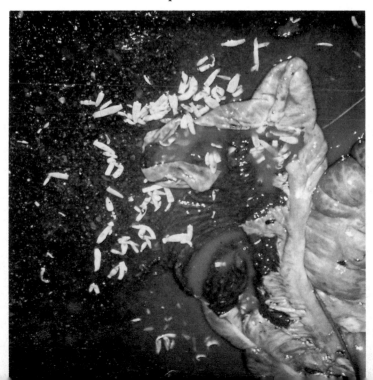

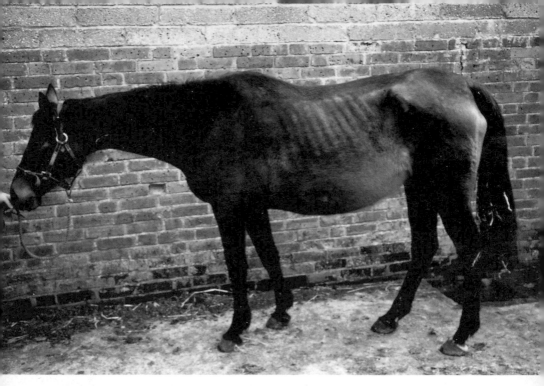

This mare is in very poor condition and scouring badly because of an infestation of red worm.

Worm infestation has caused this mare to lose condition.

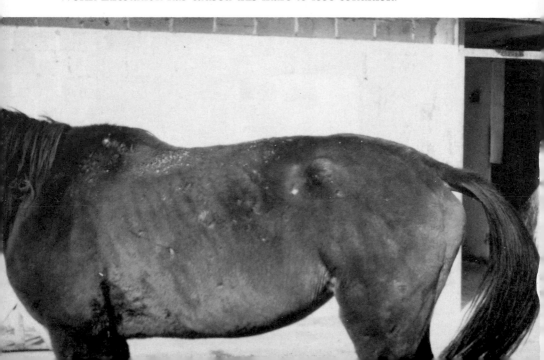

It is not good for any horse to be heavy-topped; that is, to have a body too large for its legs. If the horse does not have sufficient bone for its legs to support the weight of its body, this will obviously predispose it to leg problems. However, it is possible for a horse to appear heavy-topped simply because it is carrying too much condition, as when a light-weight is built up to look like a middleweight, or a middle-weight to look like a heavyweight.

The Shoulder

The shoulder makes all the difference to the forehand and the distribution of the horse's weight. It should start at the

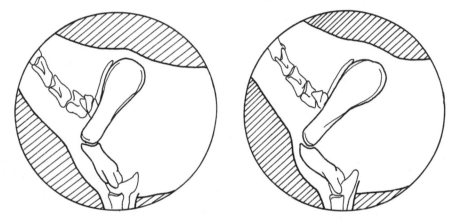

The angle of the shoulder plays an important part in the horse's freedom of movement.

A good sloping shoulder (right) allows plenty of movement and a long, sweeping stride.

With an upright shoulder (left) the range of movement of the bones is more limited and consequently the stride will be shorter. In addition the upright angles and restricted movement lessens the efficiency of the shoulder as a shock-absorber, and the increased concussion leads to greater wear and tear and the subsequent risk of unsoundness.

wither with a sloping shoulder blade covered with thick muscles which run smoothly down to the elbow. A good sloping shoulder will usually go with a sloping pastern, which enables a horse to move freely and have a good length of stride. The fetlocks will be able to act like springs, and the horse covers the ground more easily. A straight shoulder often goes with upright pasterns, which will create a shorter stride and put extra concussion onto the joints. The joints of the forelimbs, all the way from the shoulder down to the ground, act as shock-absorbers when the horse is in motion, and the more upright and less sloping the relevant angles, the less 'give' there will be in the joints and the less efficient and more restricted in their range of movement they will be.

The Forelimbs

The forearm should be long and wide, with a well-developed muscle which gradually narrows down to the knee. It is imperative for every horse that it has what is known as 'a leg at each corner'. From whatever angle you look at the horse, it should stand four square. This is especially important in the case of the forelimbs. If they should seem to 'come out of the same hole' then the width of chest will be severely restricted, and this is not a desirable feature. Not only does it mean that the horse will not have as much lung room as one with a proper width of chest, but it can lead to problems with the horse's action such as brushing or knocking of the forelimbs against one another.

The Quarters

As the hindquarters provide the driving force for the body, they must be muscular and in proportion to the rest of the frame. For a racehorse to produce speed it requires a length and depth of quarter with long straight dropped thighs and

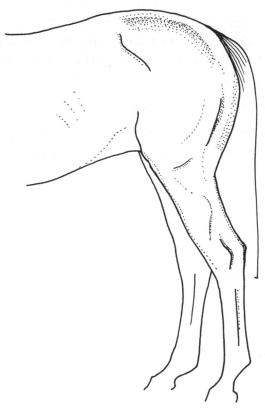

Good muscular quarters with a good strong second thigh.

hocks for strength. In any breed of horse the quarters must be muscular and well covered and should run nearly level from the croup to the dock. In addition, strong, well-muscled, nicely rounded quarters mean a well set on tail. If the quarters slope and drop away, then the tail will be low set and will not give such a nice appearance. Sloping quarters can also indicate a weak hind leg.

The Thighs

Thighs should have a good length from the stifle to the hock. They must be well muscled and the muscles on the second thigh or gaskin should be well developed. The thick tendon running down the back of the thigh from these muscles to the point of the hock is called the hamstring.

Knees and Hocks

The knee should be flat and broad with a depth from front to back to allow for the growth of strong muscles. Small round

The Thoroughbred foal (right) and Working Hunter Pony mare (left) both demonstrate the principle of 'a leg at each corner'.

knees are undesirable. The hock should be big in proportion to the size of the mare to provide strong support, and the tendons of the lower leg should run straight to the fetlock. The hocks should be strong and flexible with no puffy fillings around them.

When the horse is standing square, its weight should be evenly distributed over the four legs, and you should then be able to draw a straight line from the back of the buttock through the hock and the fetlock to the ground. You should also be able to draw a similar vertical line down through the front leg to the ground. If the front legs appear to be bent rather than straight – if the mare is over or back at the knee – or if the horse simply stands over in front, any of these could lead to leg problems and are not desirable traits to breed from.

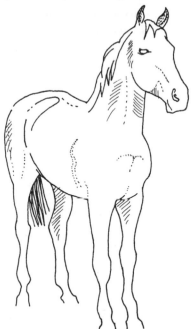

This horse, on the other hand, has forelegs which appear to 'come out of the same hole'.

Cannon Bones

The cannon bones should be short and strong with plenty of bone, and when you run the forefinger and thumb of your hand down the tendon at the back of the cannon bone it should feel well defined and straight, without a blemish. Always run your hand down the legs to check for heat or splints. There should be no swellings around the tendons, and the legs should feel cool to the touch.

Pasterns

The pasterns should be strong with a moderate length and slope. An upright pastern, as with an upright shoulder, will produce a shorter, less flexible movement and increased wear on the joints. Too long and sloping pasterns, however, may prove to be just as faulty as short, upright ones. Long pasterns do not have the strength for continuous hard work, and if a brood mare is having foals regularly, the stress on

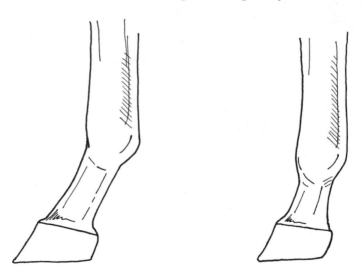

(Left) A long, weak pastern. (Right) A short, upright pastern.

the joints may eventually become so severe that she is unable to continue breeding, since the extra weight when she is heavily in foal puts additional strain on to already weakened pasterns. I remember one mare who had particularly long pasterns which did not prevent her from winning several good races as a two-year-old. However, when she was retired to stud as a four-year-old, each time she was put in foal she went down on her pasterns lower and lower until eventually, after a few years, by the time the foal was due to be born the mare's pasterns would be practically touching the ground. it was most distressing to see and of course meant in the end that the mare could no longer be bred from.

Fetlocks

These should again be large and smooth with no puffiness about them. Always avoid small, very round joints as these can be a sign of weakness.

The Hoof

This must be strong and evenly shaped with a good heel, so that the extra weight of a mare in foal does not put added strain on the tendons of the leg.

The Action

A brood mare should have a free, straight action. A long, loose, active walk is what to look for, as this is indicative of how effective her gallop would be. When she is trotted up in hand, make sure that she does not dish or plait. *Dishing* is when the foot swings outwards with each stride, and can put stress on the lower joints and thus affect performance. *Plaiting* is when the forelegs cross slightly in front of one another (hence the word 'plait') and can cause a horse to knock itself badly in trot, or in a severe case a horse could even bring itself down by tripping over its own feet. Both of these faults can be clearly seen when a horse is trotted in a straight line towards you. Neither of them, incidentally, would be acceptable in the show ring. It may be worth remembering, however, that while it is usually the result of a defect in the action, some deviation from the straight may be caused by neglected feet. In such cases this can be put right by a good farrier and no further problems should occur.

This heavyweight hunter brood mare displays a lovely swinging trot which carries her easily over the ground despite her weight.

Some defects of conformation are hereditary and it must be considered unwise to breed from a mare that might pass on these unwanted traits, such as long, weak pasterns or

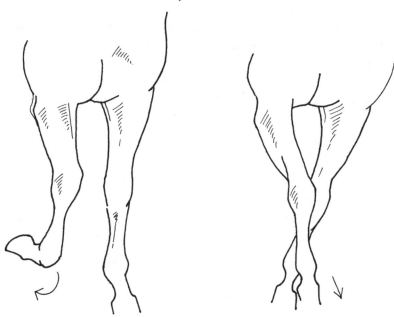

(Left) Dishing. (Right) Plaiting.

upright pasterns; being back at the knee or having weak, curvy hocks; or being too heavy-topped and too light of bone. This matter must also be thought about when looking at potential stallions. The whole question of heredity is still not fully understood, and to discuss it in depth would necessitate entering into the study of genetics outside the scope of this book. The old saying is, 'mate the best to the best', meaning that ideally a mare with good conformation, plenty of bone, good temperament and free from congenital defects, should be mated to a stallion which is well-bred and has a good record, over several seasons, of racing, jumping, eventing or whatever the particular field of competition.

Breeders have any number of theories about the matching of mare to stallion. There are, however, some basic principles of the way in which physical characteristics, temperament or ability are transmitted from parent to offspring, and these

73

determine what can and what cannot be done with a less-than-perfect animal to breed desired or undesired traits in or out respectively.

This horse has good overall conformation: a well-set-on head with a kind and generous eye; a good sloping shoulder; short cannon bones with plenty of bone below the knee; a good deep barrel giving plenty of lung room; a strong, short-coupled back; round, muscular quarters, and good sloping pasterns.

In the simplest of terms, it is generally understood that if you send a sprint-bred mare to a stoutly-bred stallion you are likely to get either a sprinter or a stayer, rather than a middle-distance performer which would be somewhere in between the two. In the same way, if you were to send a mare with short, upright pasterns to a stallion with long,

This horse has several conformation faults: an upright shoulder; long cannon bones, noticeably light of bone; short, upright pasterns, and weak, sloping quarters.

weak pasterns the resulting foal would most likely inherit either one fault or the other. If you are breeding from a mare which has rather upright pasterns, or one which is slightly heavy topped, for example, your best bet would be to send her to a stallion which has perfect conformation in that respect. It may be that you will still end up with a foal which has inherited the mare's defect, since the mare is responsible for fifty per cent of the foal's genes. However, the other fifty per cent of the foal's genetic material, contributed by the fault-free parent, will lessen the chances of the fault being passed on when the foal is bred from in turn. Every subsequent generation of the mare's family, so long as they are bred to an animal which does not itself have the defect or carry the faulty gene, will increase the chance of correcting the fault further down the generations.

The above advice should be tempered by the knowledge

that many horses with 'bad' conformation have won top events and races, and will no doubt continue to do so. Nature has a habit of proving the experts wrong on the looks and conformation of the horse or pony.

Nevertheless, the situation is much more clear-cut for breeders of show stock where conformation is critical to success, or for owners of breeds which are prone to a particular fault which the breed society is keen to eliminate. Owners of such breeds may find that a particular defect will render a mare ineligible as breeding stock with the breed society concerned, and this should be borne in mind when considering any prospective brood mare. If in doubt, always check with the authority responsible for the conditions of registration of the mare and her produce. Breeders of hunters and performance horses, for instance, should be aware that the National Light Horse Breeding Society (H.I.S.) will not accept any mare onto its Graded Register unless she is certified free of the following listed defects and diseases: cataract, bone spavin, stringhalt, sidebone, navicular disease, ringbone and shivering. Owners applying for H.I.S. registration must also declare that the mare has not been tubed, hobdayed or otherwise operated on for wind defects, or de-nerved. Acceptance onto the Grade One Register is by inspection only, and in addition to the listed defects the H.I.S. examiners will check the mare for any sign of parrot mouth, narrow or flat feet, pigeon toes, cow hocks or sickle hocks. Standards are extremely high, as the stated aim of the National Light Horse Breeding Society is to provide a register of top class mares which are capable of producing the performance horses of the future. Proven performance mares put forward for inspection will have their racing or competition record taken into account. Clearly show stock or potential competition horses which are the progeny of Grade One or Grade Two registered mares will command a higher market value, to the benefit of the breeder.

Temperament should also be taken into consideration when choosing a suitable stallion for a particular mare. While a certain amount of spirit is undoubtedly a good thing, horses which are too temperamental run a higher risk of not fulfilling their potential, since they are not always as co-operative as good-tempered ones.

A bad-tempered mare mated to an equally temperamental stallion is highly likely to produce a difficult offspring, and this should be avoided if possible. However, the way in which temperament is transmitted from parent to offspring is if anything even more complex and obscure than the transmission of conformation. It brings to mind a certain Thoroughbred mare which was the dam of a Classic winner. She was highly temperamental and was sent to a number of different stallions, producing several colts and several fillies in her lifetime. All of her colts were kind, lovable characters which won some very good races and showed no signs of the dam's temperament. All of her fillies, on the other hand, were as temperamental as the dam, and nor was their racing ability as good as the colts'.

Finally, it is probably not advisable to breed from a mare that indulges in any of the stable vices such as windsucking, crib-biting, weaving or box-walking. Although none of these is hereditary they are easily passed on to the foals, since foals learn by imitation.

The *crib-biter* bites on to the manger or edge of the stable door or the paddock rails and arches its neck, setting the neck muscles at the same time. This enables it to fill its mouth with air and swallow it, giving an audible grunt at the same time. The act of swallowing the air is what is known as *windsucking*. However, an experienced windsuck-er eventually learns to swallow air without needing to crib-bite. There is no successful remedy for either of these vices, both of which can have a deleterious effect on the digestive system and constitute an unsoundness.

A crib-biter in action. 'The crib-biter bites on to the edge of the stable door and sets its neck muscles – this enables it to fill its mouth with air and swallow it.'

Weaving is a nervous habit which can often be seen in zoos. The animal rocks itself to and fro continually when standing in its stable, sometimes lifting each front foot in turn as the body is swayed to the opposite side. It puts unnecessary stress on the front legs and can lead to lameness. Again this habit in incurable and is a habit easily learned by other horses which will copy the weaver.

Box-walking is a nervous condition in which the horse appears constantly restless and unable to stand still, circling and pacing to and fro in the box. The constant movement tires the horse unnecessarily and will adversely affect its performance. Animals with any of these vices should be kept out in the open as much as possible, since they are probably caused through boredom from spending long hours shut up in stables; and preferably away from other horses to prevent the spread of the habit.

As a general rule it is not a good idea to breed from a mare which is poor either in terms of conformation or behaviour. The aim of every breeder should be to improve the breed.

5

At Stud

This chapter looks briefly at the role of the stallion, the education of the stallion new to stud and the covering process itself, before going on to discuss the essentials of sending a mare to stud from the point of view of both the mare owner and the stallion stud.

Stallions and Covering

When a colt has reached maturity and has proved his ability in his chosen field of competition, he is ready to be sent off to stand at stud and be educated for his new job. Some stallions such as show-jumping stallions continue to compete whilst siring stock, but this is not normally an option for the Thoroughbred. In some fields of competition and in some parts of the world it is accepted practice for artificial insemination to be used to enable stallions to compete and sire stock, but this is not applicable to the Thoroughbred racehorse. No animal sired by artificial insemination will be accepted by Weatherby's for registration in the General Stud Book and such a foal would be unable to race later in life. Owners of breeds other than Thoroughbreds would be advised to check the position of their relevant breed society on artificial insemination.

The normal course of action when a new stallion arrives at stud is to turn him out in a boarded paddock for observation. He should be kept out as much as possible, especially during the off-season. His feet should be checked regularly and his shoes can be removed and the feet just trimmed thereafter, depending on what sort of work he is to be given. Time must be spent before the start of the covering season to ensure that the stallion is sufficiently fit. Some owners like their stallions to be ridden, but it is more common for them to be lunged every day or led out for long road walks as part of the fittening process. Whatever the chosen exercise, it is important to adjust the feed ration accordingly, remembering that it is not a good idea for the stallion to be overweight. Good oats and clean fresh hay should make up the majority of his diet, but a stallion which is to be used early in the year should have more protein, fed in the form of soya bean meal and lucerne hay. The protein content can then be gradually increased as the season progresses until the spring grass comes through.

At the beginning of the covering season it is the practice to take a young stallion for walks on the paths around the paddocks so that he can see a few mares and try a few of them at the 'bar'. This is made of heavy padded boards which are about 4ft (1.2m) high and strapped together along about 7ft (2.1m) of the fencing on each paddock. The mares

Teasing the mare at the bar to establish whether or not she is in season.

in the paddock are caught and brought up to the bar one at a time. The stallion is led up so that he can put his head over the bar and smell at the mare and if she is coming into use, that is to say in season, she will pass a sticky white fluid and the clitoris will wink. This will excite the stallion. Mares which are not coming into use will kick out and buck, which is why the bar needs to be well padded. The young stallion will gradually get used to the procedure, and the next stage in his education is to find an old barren mare which is well in season for him to cover.

This mare is showing signs of being well in season with hind legs apart and tail lifted high.

When the appropriate mare has been found, she should be taken into the covering yard or barn. A good floor for the covering barn is very important and worth extra expense. The ideal floor consists of a 9in (23cm) covering of tan (oak bark) on top of a chalk base. However, if this is not possible at least make sure that the surface is damped down to prevent dust. Weather conditions permitting, it is perfectly acceptable to cover outside, but this is more usual later in the summer.

A tail bandage should be put on the mare, but not a white one as this might put the stallion off, and her vulva should be opened and splashed out with warm or soapy water. Never wash a mare off with a strong disinfectant as this might upset the stallion as well as the mare. Covering boots should then be put on the mare. These are padded boots for the hind feet and will protect the stallion if the mare kicks out at him when he tries to mount her. Her near fore should be lifted up and held with a leather strap, but make sure the strap is more than 2in (5cm) wide so that it does not cut into the mare's leg.

Covering boots of felt and leather are worn on the mare's hind feet to protect the stallion from injury should she lash out at him.

A twitch can also be applied to the mare's nose as an extra means of restraint if necessary. The twitch is a small noose, the thickness of a clothes line, on the end of a pole about 2ft (.6m) long. Never use thin string to make the noose, as this could cut. The pressure on the nose releases the body's natural endorphins or painkillers and dulls the horse's senses so that it is not fully aware of what is going on. The effect is similar to that of acupuncture, and is used to calm horses that will not otherwise stand still for certain things that are done to them such as clipping, or pulling the mane. To apply a twitch, place your hand through the noose and, taking hold of the animal's muzzle, slip the noose slackly around it. Once the muzzle is in the noose, turn the pole until the noose tightens, making sure that it is never tight enough to mark the muzzle. You will know that the twitch is working when the horse's eyes go dull and sleepy and it allows you to carry out the necessary task without objection. The 2ft (.6m) pole is long enough so that the person holding it can stand clear of the front feet in case it should strike out before the twitch begins to take effect.

If a mare is exceptionally difficult to cover, it is increasingly common nowadays for her to be given a mild tranquilliser in the form of an injection administered by a veterinary surgeon. On many studs this has replaced the hobbles used previously on the most difficult mares, and sedation may well be preferable to the use of all these gadgets.

A leather pad should be placed over the mare's neck, as once the stallion has mounted he will sometimes hang on to her neck with his teeth, and this will afford her some protection. Finally when using a bar bit in the stallion's mouth use leather and not chain on the attachment to the bit.

When a young horse is covering his first mare it pays to be patient. Sometimes he may get on and off the mare two or three times without having covered her properly. Try not to keep the mare waiting longer than twenty minutes, as the stallion can always try again later on in the day. The less interference there is when a young horse is trying to cover a mare the better. Always try to do things as quietly as possible. If the horse mounts the mare wrongly try to keep the mare and stallion rotating slowly until the stallion is in the correct position. One attendant should be holding the mare by the bridle, another should hold the leg strap and a third should hold the twitch if it is needed. The stallion man helps to guide the horse's penis into the vagina and then the stallion should be left alone. The actual moment of ejaculation occurs within three minutes. A wrinkling of the quarters and the pumping action of the tail are signs that the horse is ejaculating.

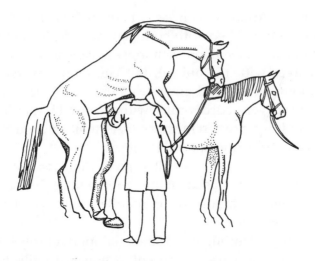

Covering. The mare is fitted with covering boots and a leather pad across her withers to protect her from the grip of the stallion's teeth. Here the stallion man is holding the mare's bandaged tail clear to facilitate entry by the stallion.

It is normal for the ejaculate to go directly into the uterus. The semen lives for a long time in the mare's genital tract – usually up to forty-eight hours although in exceptional cases it can live for up to five days. The stud groom will watch each service and if he is not satisfied he will have the mare covered again on the fourth day of her season. After the stallion has covered the mare, the penis should be washed down in a plastic jug of warm water. This is a safeguard against infection. It is best not to introduce this to a young horse until after his first two or three weeks of covering are over.

After covering the mare, it does help to sponge the stallion's front legs down once he is back in his box. Otherwise the stallion will still be able to smell the mare's sweat and her body odour and will soon excite himself.

Some young stallions do become impatient at being controlled by the stallion man when on the point of covering a mare. Accidents can easily happen. It is important that stallions are handled with both patience and firmness right from the first. A stallion man must never show fear or lose his temper with the animal, but cut short any rebellious behaviour. Horses and ponies running wild in their natural state breed very successfully without any human interference, and one must remember that stallions controlled by man have the same natural instincts.

Nevertheless, it is a sensible precaution for the stallion owner to seek insurance for any stallion in its first season to provide against him proving infertile, as this can be financially disastrous.

On a large Thoroughbred stud an important role is that of the teaser. The teaser is an entire horse, usually but not necessarily either Thoroughbred or half-bred, who has not quite made the grade to stand at stud on his own merit. His job is to test the mares at the bar in the paddocks to see if they are in season. He is a most valuable asset, as employing a teaser to take the stallion's place at the bar will save the stallion from taking too much out of himself unnecessarily during the course of a busy covering season. More often than not the teaser will get the occasional hunter mare to cover. However, on many smaller studs and non-Thoroughbred studs the stallion will do his own teasing.

The Mare at Stud

It is incumbent on any mare owner to see that the mare is clean and free from any infectious diseases* before she is sent to the stallion stud. Most studs will insist on this. A clitoral swab is needed to check that she is clear of contagious equine metritis, and a veterinary certificate to this effect must go with her to the stud. The stud may also require

* These diseases are listed and explained in full in Chapter 11.

other diseases such as Klebsiella and Pseudomonas to be checked for and a cervical swab to be taken. In some circumstances the certification required for maiden mares, barren mares and mares with foal at foot can differ slightly, and the mare owner should check with the stallion stud precisely what tests and certificates are needed.

In order to prevent the spread of contagious abortion caused by the equine herpes virus (EHV) among visiting mares, some studs will only accept in-foal mares which have been vaccinated with Pneumabort-K during their pregnancy (this procedure is explained in full in Chapter 6). Mares with foal at foot will generally be accepted whether they have been vaccinated or not.

Before being sent to stud the mare should also be wormed and should be vaccinated against equine influenza and tetanus. Her feet should be trimmed and, if she is shod, hind shoes removed. She will be spending most of her time in the paddocks outside and, if she has only recently been in work, most studs will expect her to have been 'roughed off', that is, accustomed to being turned out. She should be well-groomed and wearing a clean, strong leather headcollar with a name-plate attached to it. The stud should be informed of her arrival and if she is a Thoroughbred the mare's passport should accompany her. An in-foal mare should also be accompanied if possible by any records of her previous foalings.

In addition to the stallion fee the stallion stud will charge the mare owner for the mare's board and keep – normally a weekly rate – veterinary costs and, where appropriate, a foaling fee. Larger studs may charge a flat rate veterinary fee which covers routine attendance and most eventualities apart from exceptions such as major surgery or second opinions. Terms and conditions on public studs will vary considerably according to the size of the stud and the value of the animals to which it caters, and the stallion stud will inform the mare owner of any particular conditions that apply. For instance, while it is the practice on large Thoroughbred studs nowadays to use sedation, some stallion owners will reserve the right to use hobbles on any mare which is especially difficult to serve.

When mares are sent to the stallion stud for the covering season the paddocks selected for them should have a good growth of young grass, as this helps to bring barren and maiden mares into season. Good paddocks should also be set aside for those mares with early foals at foot.

It is often hard to tell when a young maiden mare may be coming into use, so it is a good idea to let her be seen by the teaser in the paddocks every day until she comes in season. She must then be well and truly in season before being covered. Early in the breeding season, mares that are in use may not show and the heat period may be prolonged and weak, often lasting for six to eight days or more. As the days grow longer and warmer the duration of the heat period will shorten to the normal pattern. If it is difficult to tell if a particular mare is coming in use, careful records kept of the length of each heat period should make it possible to determine the correct time. These records can also prove most helpful when trying to find the cause of barrenness in a mare which fails to conceive.

On average the normal heat period of a mare lasts for four to six days, with a three-week interval between heats. These should be regular throughout the summer, but from November to February the mare will be sexually inactive. Information in stud books and records indicates that the best days for covering a mare with a foal at foot are the second and fourth of the heat period. With barren and maiden mares the best days appear to be the third and fifth of each heat period. This system does not normally apply earlier than April, when the weather is cold and damp and the length of heat periods in barren and maiden mares can vary from eight to forty days and the average is about twelve to fifteen days long. Under these circumstances the best thing to do to save the stallion from unnecessary services is to have the mares examined by a veterinary surgeon. The alternative is to wait until April when the heat periods shorten. It is possible to inject mares with certain hormones to shorten the length of the heat periods if they are unusually long. Mares can also be injected to help bring them into season, or they can be given a product called 'Regumate' orally to help regulate their heat cycles.

On most of the busy Thoroughbred studs a veterinary surgeon is on hand every day. He usually checks each mare before covering and once she is in season. This is done by a rectal examination. The vet will insert his arm into the mare's rectum and feel for the ovaries through the rectum wall. His fingers are searching for the follicles on the ovaries: these follicles can vary in size from 32mm to 54mm and the vet can tell by feeling their size roughly how long it will be until the mare ovulates and therefore when the best time to cover her will be. Ultrasound is also now used extensively to assist in predicting ovulation.

This procedure does save the stallion from covering the mare unnecessarily and therefore wasting his energy, especially if he has a full book of mares. As the mare comes to the end of her season, there is a gap of about fourteen days before it is worth putting her to the teaser again to see whether she is coming back in use. If she does not come in season again, she can be scanned with an ultrasound scanner at sixteen days after mating to see if she is in foal. If she is in foal, or if nothing has shown but she has still failed to come in use, then she should be scanned again at thirty days and then, if she is in foal, tested manually at forty-two days to confirm the pregnancy, as there is always the risk of the embryo being reabsorbed.

Any mare that returns from the stallion stud barren at the

end of the season should undergo a thorough veterinary examination. It is very important that a reason is found for her failure to conceive. Assuming that the fertility of the stallion is not at fault, this could be anything from an infection to damage from a previous foaling to general poor condition. However, if there is an effective treatment then she will have received it well before the next covering season begins.

The Mare's Reproductive Organs

These are the vagina, the cervix, the uterus and the two ovaries. When the mare's tail is lifted up, the *vulva* can be seen. If the lips of the vulva are parted the *vagina* and the *clitoris* can be seen. The clitoris is in the part of the vagina which opens and shuts when the mare has just passed urine or when she is in season. The vagina or birth canal is separated from the uterus by the *cervix*. The cervix is relaxed when the mare comes in season to allow the

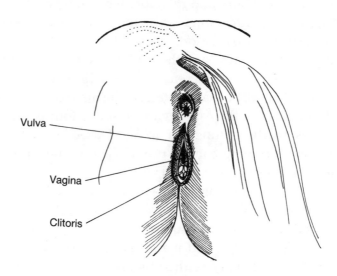

Vulva

Vagina

Clitoris

Note that under normal circumstances, when the mare is not heavily in season, the lips of the vulva would be closed.

stallion's semen to pass into the *uterus* or womb. When the mare does eventually conceive, the cervix forms a tight seal to guard against infection. The shape of the uterus is like the letter Y. The main body of the uterus is the stem of the letter and at the top of each horn of the letter is an *ovary*. When the mare comes in season one of the ovaries produces the unfertilised ovum within a *follicle*. The follicles protrude from the ovaries. Once the mare is in full season one follicle bursts and ovulation occurs. The unfertilised egg will travel slowly down the *fallopian tube*, which runs from the ovary to the horn of the uterus. The egg will meet the stallion's sperm here and fertilisation will take place. The newly fertilised egg will stay in the fallopian tube for six days before it enters the main body of the uterus. As the foetus increases in size so does the uterus right up to the time of parturition. The foetus receives all of its nourishment through the placenta and its system of blood vessels, which are connected to the wall of the uterus. The uterus is also surrounded by a layer of muscle, which is responsible for the contractions of labour.

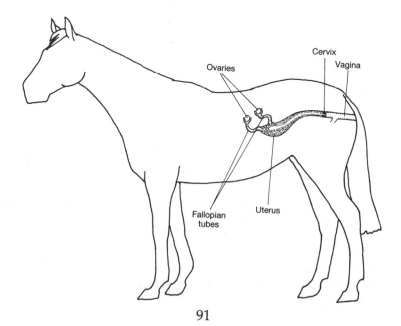

6

In-Foal Mares

A mare usually returns from stud having been covered by the selected stallion and having been scanned in-foal. Some-times, however, for reasons of expense the mare may return home before being tested forty-two days after the last service. If you have your mare at home your veterinary surgeon will carry out the necessary test for you.

Daily observation must be kept on the mare as there are such a wide range of infectious diseases from which all stud animals are at risk. One of the most devastating of these is the equine herpes virus, or EHV, which can spread like wildfire and which can cause the mare to abort. Most abortions caused by the virus occur during the ninth and tenth months of pregnancy. The EHV virus is discussed in detail in Chapter 11, Injuries and Disease, as is contagious equine metritis, another potentially serious disease with which the stallion stud may have had to deal. There are a number of other less serious bacterial and fungal infections to which mares are prone, especially as they get older. If the mare has a temperature and is obviously unwell and the vet is unable to diagnose the symptoms, blood tests and swabs will be taken from the mare to ascertain which infection is responsible.

Assuming the pregnancy is progressing without any hitches, a pregnancy certificate may be required on 1 October. This will depend on the terms agreed with the stallion stud for payment of the stallion fee, but in most cases

1 October is accepted as the date by which a mare should be certified in-foal if she has been successfully covered. (This assumes a covering season which ends on 31 July.)

Normally payment of the stallion fee will be by one of three arrangements. A straight fee is payable as soon as the mare is covered, whether she subsequently proves to be in foal or not. With a split fee, a proportion of the fee is paid on covering and the remainder is payable on 1 October, unless a veterinary certificate confirming that the mare is not in-foal is submitted on or before that date. The third system is the 'no foal, no fee' agreement, which is self-explanatory. This type of arrangement is common on most large Thoroughbred studs, where the fees the stallions command are considerable. Some studs operate concessions or refunds which may depend on the sex of the foal, or on whether or not a live foal is produced.

Whatever the arrangement agreed, it is as well to have your mare tested again at this stage in any case. It is not unknown for mares to reabsorb the foetus in the early stages of pregnancy.

If the mare is a Thoroughbred maiden mare it will be time to have her blood-typed for the Weatherby's brood mare register. Weatherby's will send a blood kit and identity form for the veterinary surgeon to complete – do be certain to return the blood sample promptly after it has been taken. It is also time to have the mare vaccinated against the equine herpes virus, using a drug called Pneumabort-K. This is administered by multiple injections during the fifth, seventh and ninth months of the mare's pregnancy. It is worthwhile vaccinating any barren mares in contact with the in-foal mares to prevent the spread of the virus if it occurs. Remember that other forms of infectious diseases are still a danger to the pregnant mare, and even once she has been vaccinated against EHV constant observation is still essential.

When the mare arrives back at the owner's stud or stable in good health and in-foal, she should be turned out with the other in-foal mares. However, she may be the only pregnant mare and in this case a companion must be found for her. An old retired horse or pony will suffice and will help the mare to settle down more quickly. Later the companion will help a great deal when the time for weaning the foal comes around. At this time the mare is taken as far away from the foal as possible, so that they cannot hear each other calling, and it is much less stressful for the foal if it has another animal which it is used to for company. A donkey is not really an acceptable companion as it is possible for the mare to contract lung worm and liver fluke from the donkey's faeces.

In-foal maiden mares are sometimes highly strung and do not relax and settle down as quickly as older brood mares. It helps to visit the mare as often as possible in these circumstances, so that she can gain a bit of confidence. This is especially important if the mare is to foal at home as the familiar voice of the handler will help to calm her when she is foaling and in an agitated condition. The mare can be left out day and night from April to October, but of course this does depend on the environment, weather, shelter and the amount of available grazing.

An experienced horse person can soon tell if the mare is not quite herself. However, an inexperienced person who is sent to look at the mare should have some idea of what to look for. If the mare is standing still, move her on for a few strides, as there is always a possibility that she might be lame. If she looks a bit dull, bring her in and take her temperature. If she is lying down and it seems a pity to disturb her, she must still be got to her feet as she might be lame or she might have a touch of colic, in which case she would get down again immediately. Another cause of discomfort can be the foetus moving inside the mare, in which case the mare will get down and roll until she moves the foetus and feels more comfortable.

Other things to watch out for are whether the mare is showing signs of stress, such as sweating or breathing heavily, or whether she has suffered any cuts or kicks as these should always be treated at once. Swollen glands on either side of the throat, and dirty noses – mucus secretion from one or both nostrils – should always be taken very seriously indeed, as these may be the first signs of a virus.

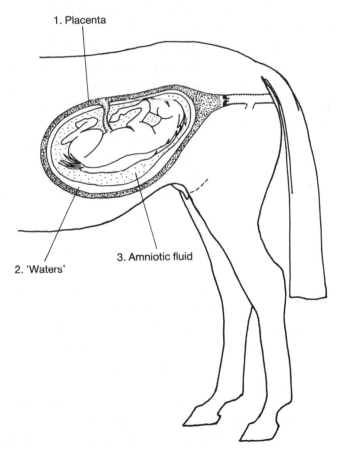

1. Placenta

2. 'Waters'

3. Amniotic fluid

The fully developed foetus in the womb.

Discharge from the vagina must also not be ignored. Any of these problems should easily be noticed during the day-to-day handling of the mare. More vigilance is required in the summer when she is permanently out at grass, so that nothing is overlooked.

The gestation period of the horse is eleven months. The last service date, which is the date when the stallion last covered the mare, is the date from which the approximate date of foaling can be calculated. Thus if the last service date was 14 March, the mare's foaling date will be 14 February. These dates are only a rough guide, however, as it is quite possible for the mare to foal two to three weeks prematurely or even two or three weeks late without any ill effects to either mare or foal.

Before the mare is due to foal a decision must be taken about whether she is to foal at home or at the stallion stud. Some owners prefer to have their mare at home to foal down. This is quite understandable as it is a very exciting moment. However, if the owner wants the mare covered on the foaling heat, which will happen seven to nine days after the foaling, consideration must be given to the distance the mare and newly-born foal would have to travel to the stallion stud. A long-distance journey by horse-box can be very stressful and tiring for a young foal. It might become chilled in an over-warm horse-box or even catch a virus in an alien environment. Also, once the mare is in season the change in the composition of her milk is likely to cause the foal to scour, and this would further weaken the foal after a long journey.

Alternatively the mare can be sent away to foal at the stallion stud, which obviously lessens the risks to the young foal. It is advisable to send the mare away about one month before she is due to foal. This will enable her to acclimatise to her new environment, so that she is not stressed herself at

This mare is well in season.

Stallion mounting the mare ready to cover.

Stallion man putting the penis in the mare.

Stallion on the point of ejaculation.

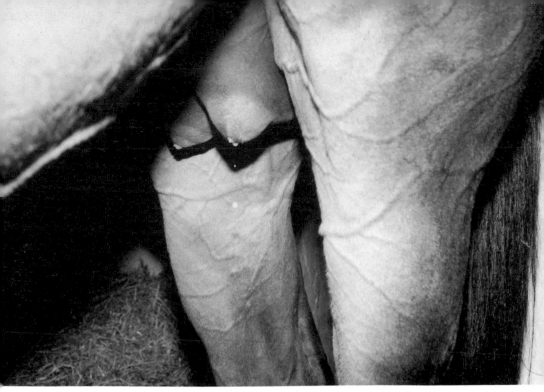

The following photographs illustrate normal foaling. (*Above*)
The mare has bagged up and waxed up. A drop of milk has
started to trickle from the bag. (*Below*) She breaks water and the
foal's front feet appear.

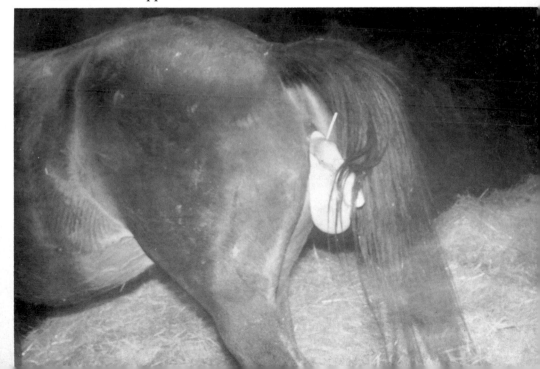

(Above and below) The mare gets down as the contractions become much stronger.

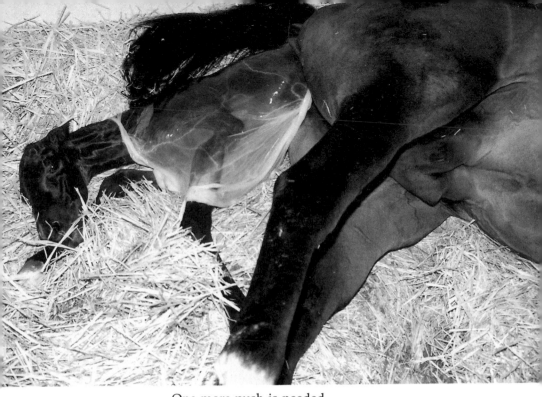

One more push is needed.

The foal still attached to the umbilical cord.

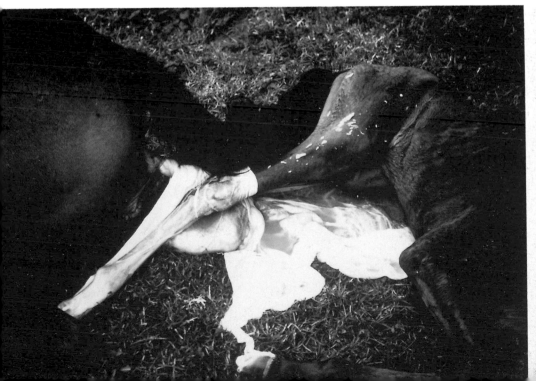

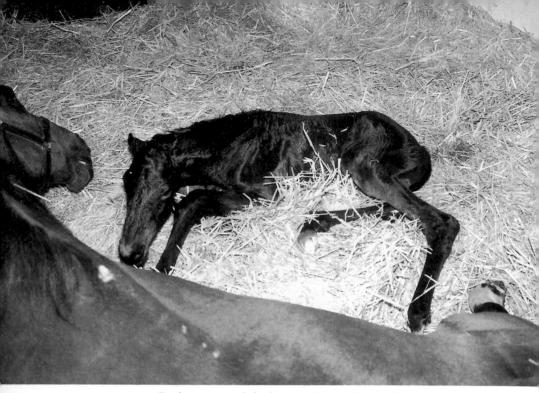

Both mare and foal are rather exhausted.

Introducing the foal to the udder.

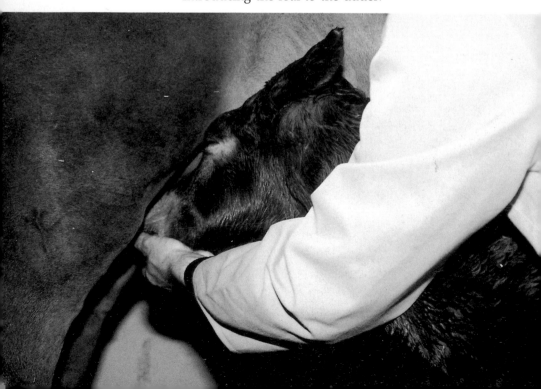

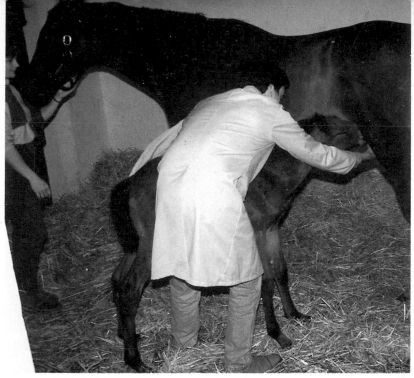

Some assistance is needed as the foal is still weak on its legs.

The bottom half of the afterbirth being lifted and tied up with string.

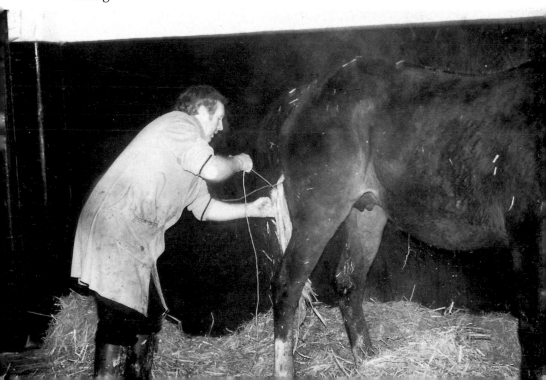

Eight hours after foaling the bonding of mare and foal is complete.

Thoroughbred yearlings standing in mock starting stalls.

the time of foaling. Of course to board the mare at the stallion stud for those extra weeks will incur additional expense, which may be a consideration for the small breeder.

For those owners who would prefer to have their mare foal down at home and yet want to take advantage of the foaling heat, artificial insemination could be the answer. However, it has already been explained in Chapter 5 that this is not possible for the Thoroughbred racehorse, and may not be permissible in other breeds. If you are satisfied that artificial insemination will not disqualify your mare's produce from the Stud Book or other register of the breed concerned and wish to take this option, your veterinary surgeon should be able to advise on the necessary arrangements.

7

Foaling

The aim of this chapter is to describe what to expect at each stage of a normal, healthy foaling. Obviously no two foalings are the same, but these general guidelines should explain the normal course of events.

As the mare progresses into the last weeks of her pregnancy, careful watch should be kept on her mammary glands or milk glands. These will gradually swell until they look heavy. This stage is known as 'bagging up' and indicates that the mare will foal within the next few days. A mare who has had a previous foal will have a larger bag than a maiden mare, but the maiden mare's bag will develop as the foal sucks.

About a day before the mare foals a waxy substance will be secreted from the teat of each udder. It looks very much like candle grease and this stage is known as 'waxing up'. If the mare is seen to be running milk the birth is imminent. One precaution which must not be overlooked is that if the mare starts to run milk while she is waxing up, a note should be taken of the length of time that the mare ran milk before foaling. Only the first milk from the mare contains colostrum and it is critical that the foal receives this within the first few hours of its birth. Colostrum is rich in infection-fighting antibodies and without them the foal will have no natural immunity from disease in the first few months of its life. If the mare has run milk for more than a few hours before foaling, the veterinary surgeon should be consulted, as extra colostrum will be needed by the foal to replace that which was lost.

Some of the larger studs may keep their own store of colostrum. Colostrum freezes well, and if a foal is born dead it is possible to milk the mare and store the colostrum-rich milk in a freezer for future use. It is perfectly possible for the small owner with one or two mares at home to do this. However, it must be done quickly as only the first milk of the mare contains the colostrum, and if she is not milked straight away the mare will run the milk of her own accord and the colostrum will be wasted.

Before the mare foals it is advisable to check whether she has been stitched. This means that part of the vulva, the entrance to the mare's genital tract, was stitched while she was away at the stallion stud. This is done only if the mare is sucking air into her uterus through an abnormally slack vulva and is a precaution taken in such cases to prevent chronic infection, which could prevent the mare from conceiving. The scar, which can be clearly seen, should only be about 1 to 1½in (2.5 to 3.7cm) long and it should be reopened by a veterinary surgeon a day or two before the mare is due to foal. If the mare does start to foal before this is done, it is possible to cut along the scar with a pair of surgical scissors. No painkilling injection is required, as this is old scar tissue. If this is done in time it will stop the vulva from tearing when the foal is born and it can be stitched up again the day after the mare has foaled.

The majority of mares foal at night, when conditions are much quieter. Presumably this is nature's way when the mares are with a herd in the wild. The mare would foal at night and the foal would then have a chance to strengthen up before following its dam with the rest of the herd the next day. Statistics have shown that eighty-six per cent of mares foal at night between 7pm and 7am with fifty per cent of this group foaling within the two hours either side of midnight. The remaining fourteen per cent of mares can foal at any time of the day or night.

Before the mare foals a large box should be scrubbed down and disinfected. Once this has been done it can be bedded up with plenty of fresh, dust-free long wheat straw. Some sort of provision should be made to supply extra heat to the box in the event of a sickly foal being born. There must also be access to hot water and a telephone for the attendant. On the more lavish studs there will be a bedsit for the person who is supervising the mare constantly until she foals.

In warmer weather, between May and September, mares can foal outside quite safely, but it must be possible to keep an eye on them, so keep them nearby in a small handy paddock. Obviously even in summer any mare who is due to foal should be brought in if the weather turns unduly wet or cold. Up until May the foaling must take place in a stable. Normally it is common practice to foal Thoroughbreds under cover as they usually foal down early in the year.

It is always an apprehensive time when a mare starts to foal as nobody knows what will happen during the birth. Some mares can foal very easily and without any complications, whilst others may have problems with a badly presented foal, which causes added stress to the mare and necessitates extra attention from the attendant at the birth.

Foaling mares can be very unpredictable. A mare can be standing in the paddock grazing one moment, looking very relaxed, with a large blob of wax on her teats, and then five minutes later she is lying prostrate on the ground having her foal. Another mare might be uncomfortable and pace around for two or three hours before foaling. Some mares can even be unsettled all day and yet still not foal until night time. If a mare has foaled before, it is advantageous to keep a record of her previous foalings, as this can help to give a good indication of what to expect.

Vigilance is the key word when waiting for a mare to foal. When she has bagged up and waxed up, perhaps has a drop of milk running from her teat and may be looking slightly uncomfortable, then it is time to put a tail bandage on the mare and make sure that the skirt of her tail is not too long. If it is necessary to trim an over-long tail so that it does not get in the way it is advisable to use long scissors, so that you do

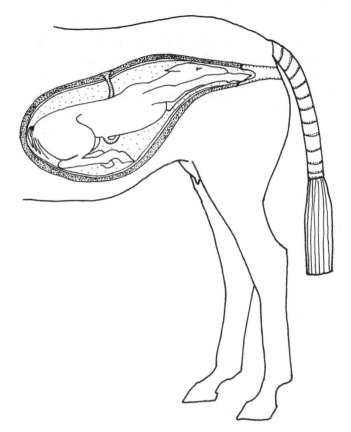

The foal has rotated into the correct position for delivery. The waters have broken and the mare's tail is bandaged in preparation for the birth.

not get a chopped, uneven look. It is not necessary to cut the tail so short as to spoil the appearance of the mare. The ideal length for any horse's tail is on a level with the chestnut, and if you do have to cut the tail it is helpful to have one person hold their arm under the dock so that the tail hangs naturally while another person cuts it to the right length.

The mare should be observed discreetly and without disturbance and she should be kept as quiet as possible. She may be eating hay when she gets her first pain and she will probably walk around the box and then proceed to eat again. The next pain that comes will be a little more vigorous than the last and will take longer to pass, and again she may walk round the box and maybe scrape at the straw in annoyance and perhaps pass a few droppings. The pains will start to come more frequently and be more severe and at this stage she may break sweat or get down as though suffering with colic. Some mares sweat more than others and some hardly sweat at all. She will then get up again and stand ready to stale or urinate; this is when the waterbag inside her bursts and the waters gush out. A note should be taken of the time when this happens, as the birth should be complete within the next forty minutes.

The mare will now get down once more and have her first contractions. At this stage it is advisable to put your hand into the vaginal tract and feel that the front feet of the foal are straight and that its head is lying on its feet. If the head and feet are in the correct position it is best to leave the mare alone. It must be remembered that quietness throughout is essential and just one attendant at this stage is quite sufficient. As the mare continues to have her contractions the feet of the foal will appear and the mare may get up again and walk around the box: this may be to help position the foal correctly. Attention must be paid when she does this in case she should get down with her hind quarters facing into the corner of the box, as this might restrict the delivery of the foal. If this does happen it is advisable to move the mare back to the centre of the box: this is one of the reasons why it is essential to use large foaling boxes to help avoid such eventualities.

With the next contraction the head of the foal will appear. Both the head and feet will be enveloped in a fine membrane, which is called the *chorion*. It looks very much like a piece of clear plastic. Usually the foal's feet can be seen sticking through the membrane, but occasionally the membrane may be a bit stronger and the attendant will just have to break it and lift it over the foal's head and legs. The last contraction, and the strongest, will push the rest of the foal right out on to the straw.

The foal will start to breathe immediately and soon try to move. The mare will lie still for a short period of time, a little exhausted. It is important that they are still at this time as the foal is still attached to the mare by the umbilical cord and the rest of the foal's blood is being pumped into its body from the placental membrane by way of this cord. When the mare does eventually get to her feet the cord will break and it is at this point that the foal's umbilicus must be dressed with an antibiotic powder to prevent infection. The foal's air passages can also be checked for obstructions and one can make sure that its eyelids are not turned down.

When the mare gets to her feet she will turn to look at the foal and start to lick it. The foal in its turn will try to get to its feet but will probably fall over. After several attempts to do so, the foal should be standing within about an hour. Its suck reflex will be evident now and it will try to suck anywhere on the mare until it finds the udder or is introduced to it. As this can take at least an hour or so, help from the attendant is often important. The mare should be held and the foal quietly guided in the direction of the mare's hind legs.

Patience is needed as the foal is still a bit weak on its legs and the mare may become unsettled if she cannot see the foal. It is advisable to let the mare keep in close contact with the foal and to let her lick its hind quarters if she wants. Sometimes a more experienced mare will gently push the foal in the right direction herself. It is vital that the attendant makes absolutely sure that the foal sucks and that it has a good drink, as this is the critical colostrum intake. Once the foal has had its first suck the bonding of mare and foal is complete.

After the foal has had a good drink it will strain to pass its first droppings, which are known as the *meconium*. The meconium is a sticky brown mass of faeces accumulated in the rectum while the foal is in the womb. If the foal continues to strain without passing anything for the next hour or so an enema should be given to avoid meconium impaction. Removal of the meconium, should it prove necessary, is described more fully in Chapter 8. A watch should also be kept to check that the foal urinates without problem and to see that the urine is a healthy colour: if it is darkish brown or red this indicates a kidney disorder and a veterinary surgeon should be called.

Special attention should be given to the mare and foal to see that they have not suffered any injury or trauma during the birth. When the mare gets to her feet after the foal is born the afterbirth will hang out of the mare and sometimes drag on the floor. In this case the bottom half of the afterbirth can be lifted and tied up to the top with a bit of string until such time as the entire afterbirth comes away on its own. On no account should any attempt be made to cut or pull the afterbirth away from the mare as this could result in damage to the inside of the mare. If the afterbirth has not come away within ten to twelve hours, a veterinary surgeon should be called to remove it. Once the afterbirth has been dropped, the placenta should be laid out flat on the floor to see if any part has been torn or left inside the uterus. The opening from which the foal emerged will be clearly seen and at the opposite end are two protruding horn shapes; one horn will be intact and the other, which is the pregnant horn, will be torn or split. If any other part is torn or missing or there are any diseased or thickened areas then a vet should be called.

Sometimes after foaling the mare may get down to have a rest. She might still feel uncomfortable and almost appear to have colic pains as the uterus contracts. It is advisable to check her pulse: the normal pulse rate for a mare is between thirty-four and forty beats per minute. The pulse should be regular and strong. If it is weak the mare could have problems such as internal haemorrhaging (this is more common with older mares) or a haematoma (blood clot). Whatever the problem a veterinary surgeon should be called and the mare kept as quiet as possible until his arrival. In the event of a tragedy the vet should also be able to arrange for a foster mare.

If the mare shows no sign of discomfort she should be given a warm bran mash to eat and chilled water to drink. The wet and soiled straw should be taken out of the box and replaced with clean, fresh straw. Finally when the mare and foal are more settled it is a good idea to sponge out the mare's eyes and nose and her hind quarters, as this will freshen her up; but all the time she must be allowed to remain close to her foal. The attendant must do all this very quietly in order not to upset either mare or foal.

Maiden mares foaling for the first time can be totally different to older brood mares, which is understandable as they have no idea what is going on when they are foaling. Some maiden mares can get very frightened and extremely upset as the labour pains increase and may even throw themselves about, getting up and down, rolling and sweating profusely. Then after the foal is born and the mare sees it for the first time, she can get very panicky as she cannot understand what she has got in the box with her. It can take a very long time for a maiden mare to accept the foal, especially when the foal gets to its feet and is introduced to her. She may kick out at it and back away from it, but with a lot of talking and soothing from the attendant she will take to it eventually.

A maiden mare may even resent the foal trying to suckle, and again, a great deal of patience is required to soothe her. The best course of action is to catch the mare and hold up one of her front legs to stop her from kicking while someone else guides the foal to her teats. She will probably squeal when she feels the foal sucking, but after a while she will settle down.

As a general note it is important at this stage to make sure the foal suckles from both teats, as this will prevent mastitis.

The Healthy Foal

Temperature of normal foal: 99–101°F (37.2–38.3°C).

Pulse rate: 50–80 beats per minute, rising to
120–140 per minute after one hour, falling to
80–120 per minute after twelve hours.

Normal respiration rate: 70 per minute, falling to
35 per minute within the first twelve hours.

8

Foaling Problems and Foal Abnormalities

Some of the difficulties which can occur during and immediately after foaling are described in this chapter, to help the mare owner to realise when the foaling is not going smoothly, and to know when to call for veterinary assistance. It should be stressed that if you have any doubts at all then it is essential that you contact your veterinary surgeon.

Before Foaling

When a mare is starting to foal and the attendant feels inside the birth canal to check that the foal is correctly positioned, he may find that the foal's fetlock joints are bent under, rather than pointing straight forward; or he may find that the feet are pushing up into the roof of the canal and causing damage to the mare. Either of these situations must be rectified at once. The attendant must feel for the legs whilst the mare is resting between contractions and then bring the feet forward into the correct position. Once this is done, the next time the mare has a contraction the foal will move forward unhindered.

A foal can be presented upside down, but with some help both the mare and foal should be all right. If a foal is presented backwards, however, it must be removed as soon as possible and obviously this is a case for the veterinary surgeon. If the placenta comes first this must be broken and the attendant must help the mare by gently pulling on the foal's legs every time the mare pushes. In some cases the mare pushes out the uterus with the foal. If this happens the uterus should be supported until the vet arrives.

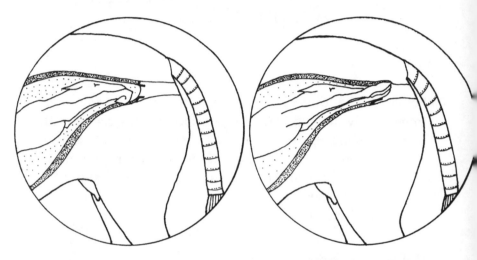

If the foal's fetlocks are bent under (left) or if the feet are pushing up into the roof of the birth canal, a careful and experienced attendant should be able to rectify the situation. Any other problems of incorrect presentation will require immediate veterinary intervention.

Obviously it is possible for the foal to be stillborn, but in some cases the heart is beating even though the foal is not breathing, or at least there is no sign of breathing through the nostrils. The attendant should blow hard up one nostril several times at five-second intervals, until the foal starts to breathe on its own.

In instances where it proves necessary to call the veterinary surgeon, it is advisable to put a bridle on the mare and walk her around the box until his arrival.

After Foaling

Some foals are born with nervous disorders. Fortunately such disorders are not common, but nevertheless they do from time to time occur.

Barking foals can start life quite normally for the first twenty-four hours and then they start having nervous twitches or convulsive seizures, during which they make noises rather like a barking fox: short, sharp barks or yaps often in pairs and recurring at varying intervals. In severe cases the foal will fall on its side and make galloping movements with both front and hind legs, until it is exhausted. No time should be lost in seeking veterinary attention, and every effort must be made to contain and control the convulsions by holding on to the foal's feet. If the foal is standing, try to place its quarters into a corner to control its movements. Talk to the foal quietly and try to soothe it while waiting for the vet to arrive.

Wanderers are foals which wander about the box as if blind. They have no idea about sucking or drinking and so are in need of continual nursing. Similarly *dummy foals* seem to be all right in every respect apart from the fact that they will not suck. The prognosis for them is good. The treatment for these disorders consists of administering sedatives and ensuring that the foal is kept warm and quiet. Milk has to be given by a veterinary surgeon, using a stomach tube. It is not a good thing for a foal to drink from a pan or bucket during the early stages, as it will prove difficult to persuade it to suck the teat thereafter. When the foal is stronger it can be fed from a bottle until it is ready to move on to feeding on its own from the mare.

Some foals may look very weak and wobbly at birth, as though premature. They must be watched very carefully in case the wobbliness is caused by a spinal disorder. Some of the mildest cases recover quickly, but more serious ones may take seven to ten days of treatment before they are right. Vigilant nursing is really the key to recovery from any of these problems and it involves very long hours.

Premature Foals

Foals have little chance of survival if they are born more than three weeks early. A premature foal must be kept warm. It needs to be fed every hour and to do so it must sit up on its chest and be given about a quart of milk, which has been milked from the mare, in a bottle with a teat. The sort of bottle a shepherd uses to feed a lamb is ideal. The mare can be expected to give up to three gallons of milk every twenty-four hours.

The foal must be turned every hour for its circulation. A rug should be placed over it for warmth, making sure that the rug is not too heavy, and its legs should be bandaged to help conserve body heat. Great care must be taken whenever a foal's legs are bandaged not to damage the circulation. Gamgee gauze must first be wrapped around the leg and then the bandage applied, making sure that it is not too tight.

Twins

Twins are rare these days, especially from Thoroughbred mares, as the mare can be scanned for early pregnancy and twin diagnosis by ultrasound. The ultrasound probe is inserted into the rectum and allows visualisation of the embryo as early as twelve to fourteen days. If twins are detected it is possible to inject the mare with prostaglandin to abort her, and cover her again in the same season – or it may be possible to squeeze one of the foals at seventeen to twenty days.

In any case mares rarely manage to carry twins full term, and the majority will abort naturally from four months onwards. In a few cases one live foal will survive, which would normally be small and weak and require the same sort of attention as a premature foal.

However, if twins are successfully delivered, the mare is quite capable of supporting them, provided she has plenty of milk. One twin is often much smaller than the other. If the foals do not seem to thrive, a milk supplement is available to provide the necessary additional nourishment and can be fed from a bottle with a teat until they are old enough to drink from a pan or bucket.

Stillborn Foals

In the unfortunate event of a stillborn foal, a careful watch should be kept on the mare in case she should develop mastitis (an infection of the mammary glands which is explained in Chapter 11). It helps to express a small amount of milk from the mare, but she should dry up naturally within a few days.

Congenital Abnormalities

These can be seen immediately after the birth, but are not always necessarily as serious as they may at first appear.

Legs: the fetlock joints may be abnormally straight either because of the length of tendon or because of the pastern. If the foal can stand after the birth then it is possible that the joints will right themselves in a few days, in much the same way as the foal will come up on its pasterns in due course. However, if the foal buckles as it stands then a veterinary surgeon should be called at once, and the foal should be put on short bedding or chaff as this provides

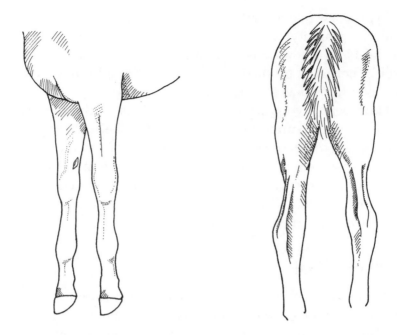

Limb abnormalities such as contracted tendons, which will give the appearance of upright fetlocks (left) or twisted hind legs (right), can improve dramatically in the first few weeks of the foal's life. Your vet will advise on the necessary course of action.

an easier surface for it to move on. If one or other of the hind legs is twisted, the best thing to do is to put the mare and foal out in a paddock as soon as possible, for the legs will stand a better chance of improving if exercised. It is best not to take too pessimistic a view of the situation at this stage with hind leg abnormalities, as the foal has considerable ability to correct minor deformities naturally. It is astonishing how some quite alarming-looking defects can rectify themselves in this manner. Only if there is no improvement in a few days should it be necessary to call a veterinary surgeon. Knock-kneed foals are a different matter altogether. This may be improved by an operation, and a veterinary surgeon

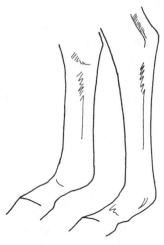

It is natural for a foal which is 'down on its pasterns' at birth to rise up on them in due course when the pasterns have strengthened.

should be called to assess the severity of the condition as soon as possible.

Mouth: the foal's jaw should be checked for a parrot mouth deformity. This is when the top teeth or gums protrude over the bottom teeth or gums. The exact opposite is known as an undershot jaw. Some cases are more pronounced than others and the worst cases may find it very difficult to graze on short grass as they have no bite. However, with a corn-fed foal, it should make no difference to how well it does and should not affect the animal's performance in later life. A cleft palate will show when the foal is drinking from the mare, as the milk will come back down out of the foal's nose. This can be very serious and the advice of the veterinary surgeon should be sought at once.

Internal Problems

During the first few days attention must be paid to whether the foal urinates easily. A foal which is experiencing difficulty could be suffering from a ruptured bladder or a severe bladder inflammation caused by bacteria infecting the navel which may have failed to heal after the birth. In both of these cases it is imperative that the advice of a vet is sought immediately.

When the foal is born there are firm, black balls of faeces in the colon and rectum. These are known as the meconium and it is most important that they are passed as quickly as possible. If the foal fails to do so it will soon show signs of pain, almost like a colic. An enema of liquid paraffin will help to ease the blockage and in some cases it may be necessary to extract the faeces manually, when great care must be taken not to damage the rectum. This complaint seems to be especially common in large colt foals and requires veterinary attention.

Rupture can arise in a colt foal shortly after the birth. It will cause a large, soft swelling to form between the hind legs. Most ruptures will go away without any intervention. This is not the case, however, with an umbilical hernia, which forms

An umbilical hernia will require veterinary attention.

at the navel. It is caused by a piece of gut being pulled with the umbilical cord at the time of foaling. Occasionally the gut will go back on its own, but more often it becomes quite large and an operation is required to push it back. Obviously this cannot be done until the foal is strong enough to undergo an operation. If the hernia hardens during a short space of time, it may mean that an abscess is forming. This could be very serious and veterinary advice is necessary.

Infections

If the mare is known to have *haemolytic anaemia* or 'yellow jaundice', the foal should be kept off her for thirty-six hours after birth and should be kept as quiet as possible. If the foal is allowed to suck from the mare during this period the disease may be passed on to the foal via the antibodies in the mare's colostrum. The mare should be milked by hand every two to three hours to remove the colostrum. A veterinary surgeon will advise and give artificial protection to the foal in the form of antibiotics if an alternative source of colostrum from a colostrum bank is not available. It is, however, very important to try to ensure that there is an alternative source of colostrum.

If the foal has sucked from the mare, a change could be noticed in its demeanour at any time from within the first six hours until as late as five days afterwards. The foal will be very tired and sleepy and its urine will be a dark red colour. It is impossible to tell a jaundiced foal at first sight, as the foal is quite normal at birth and it is only after the first suck that it will start to show signs of the disease. It does not run a temperature, but the heart rate goes up to sixty beats per minute and it is possible to hear the heart beat when standing in the box. The breathing rate increases also and the top lip turns yellow. In extremely bad cases the foal's blood might have to be changed, but prevention of the disease is the best course of action. The next time the mare is due to foal she must have a blood test to determine whether she is carrying the disease again and to ensure that the foal does not contract it.

Septicaemia can be caused by the mare running milk for days before foaling, so that by the time the foal has its first suck all the colostrum has already leaked away, giving the foal no immunity to infection. This is very serious and must be treated with a course of antibiotics.

Joint-ill is another condition which requires immediate attention. The infected blood carries the bacteria to the joints, where the bacteria eventually form pus. Any form of lameness in a very young foal should be regarded as a suspected case of joint-ill. The best method of prevention is to ensure that the navel is regularly dressed with antibiotic powder and that the foal's box is kept clean: in short, good husbandry.

Foster Mares

If the worst should happen and you should lose the mare, you will need to find a foster mare for the foal. Your veterinary surgeon may know of any that are likely to be available, for instance if a mare on a nearby stud has lost her foal. There is also an organisation called the National Foaling Bank which is unique to Britain and which operates a twenty-four-hour emergency service to put breeders in touch with available foster mares in all parts of the country. Full details of the National Foaling Bank can be found in Appendix III. They may also be able to advise on alternative sources of colostrum and milk powder for foals if necessary.

It used to be common practice, if the foster mare had only just lost her own foal, to skin the dead foal and put the skin over the foal to be fostered, so that the foster mare would smell her own foal rather than the scent of a stranger. Another method of familiarising the foster mother to the orphaned foal is to smear a little of the mare's milk on the foal's face so that she will smell herself on it and so take to it more readily.

9

General Welfare of Mare and Foal

The First Few Days

Some mares are very possessive of their foals and the first few days can be rather difficult. In extreme cases the mare may not even let the attendant in the box, but more usually they continually put themselves between the foal and the attendant, thereby hiding the foal and preventing the attendant from checking on it. These cases have to be dealt with patiently and kindly, but firmly, as it is important that the foal should be well handled from day one onwards.

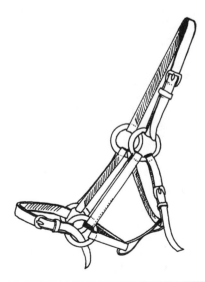

Foal slip.

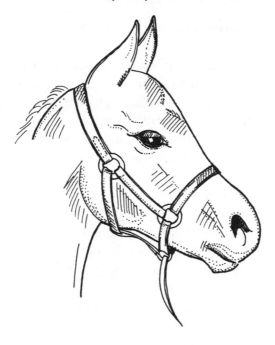

Foals grow fast, and once fitted the foal slip should be checked regularly and adjusted accordingly to make sure it does not become too tight.

On the second or third day after foaling a tetanus anti-toxin injection should be administered. The foal should also be fitted with a leather foal slip. The slip must be checked regularly as the foal grows so fast that the slip will frequently need altering to prevent it rubbing the foal. Once the slip is fitted the mare and foal can be led out on the third day, providing the foal is strong enough and the weather conditions are suitable. It is preferable if the grass is not wet. There is no point in leading them out if conditions are not favourable as the foal is particularly vulnerable to the cold at this time of its life. Obviously this is more of a problem with Thoroughbreds as they tend to foal earlier in the year when the weather is not so likely to be good. If it is not possible to lead them out, do make sure that the mare is not over-fed while she and her foal are confined to the box.

When they are led out it is advisable to lead the mare on a bridle rather than a headcollar to begin with as she may be feeling a bit lively after standing in for a few days, and it is useful to have an extra pair of hands to help with the foal. It is important to start getting the foal to move around so that it can rise up on its pasterns, and the exercise will help this essential process. The mare can graze on the bridle while the foal can roam around freely in the nursery paddock.

After a few days it should be possible to let the mare go as well, as at this point it is a good idea to turn them out in a small nursery paddock, which will ensure that the mare will not be able to gallop about. It is important to try and prevent her from doing so as the foal is still unbalanced and it might not be able to turn away from the railings as fast as the mare. Quiet grazing in the nursery paddock will also give the mare a chance to settle down with her foal before being turned out with the other mares. The first few days are nerve-racking as the foal seems so vulnerable, but in reality foals are extremely strong and usually progress in leaps and bounds. In fact their strength should not be underestimated and extra care must be taken not to be in the firing line of their flying little hooves.

After a few days, mare and foal can be turned out together in a small nursery paddock.

The mare will come into season for her foaling heat about seven to ten days after foaling. The foal may scour at this time and this can be counteracted by administering a suspension of internal protectants orally. The product, which is called 'Stat', can be obtained from your veterinary surgeon. If possible Vaseline should be applied to the foal's

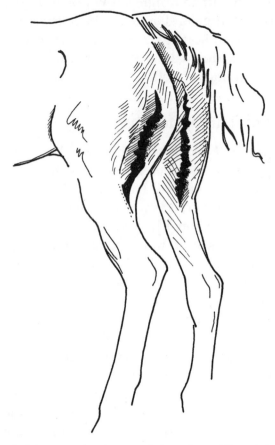

If a scouring foal is not properly attended to, the acidity of the diarrhoea will burn the hairs of the coat and will not only cause discomfort but may, as on this foal, result in a large area of bare skin and semi-permanent scarring. Clean the foal frequently and apply a protective layer of Vaseline to the inside of the hindquarters to minimise discomfort and damage.

hind legs and buttocks before it begins to scour. The excreta will run down the foal's hind legs and without the protection of the Vaseline will dry and scald the hair underneath, causing it to fall off and leaving a bare patch of skin which is unnecessary, unsightly and uncomfortable for the foal. If the scouring continues for several days and the excreta changes colour to a light brown or nearly white shade, a veterinary surgeon should also be called in to deal with any possible complications. A veterinary surgeon should also be called in if the foal stops sucking, becomes depressed or starts grinding its teeth.

One to Three Months

At one month old Thoroughbred foals should have a blood sample taken in order for the foal to be registered with Weatherby's, who will have sent a blood-typing kit to the owner of every expectant mare before she is due to foal. The blood sample cannot be taken until the foal is a month old and once taken it must be dispatched to Weatherby's immediately. No foal will be accepted for registration until the blood samples have been successfully analysed. On completion of registration all Thoroughbred foals born in Great Britain and Ireland are issued with a foal passport which has replaced the foal identity and vaccination certificate issued previously and remains valid throughout the animal's racing and breeding career.

Blood samples are not usually required to register foals with other breed societies, although some, such as the Arab Horse Society, may reserve the right to require blood typing to substantiate the identity of the animals concerned if necessary before a passport or registration certificate is issued. Responsible breeders should obviously check the procedure for the registration of foals with the breed society concerned in good time. The Arab Horse Society for example stipulates that all foals, whether Pure Bred, Anglo-Arab or Part Bred, must be examined by a veterinary surgeon for registration purposes before the foal is four months old, in other words, while the foal is still on the mare. The addresses and telephone numbers of several of the major breed societies are listed in Appendix IV.

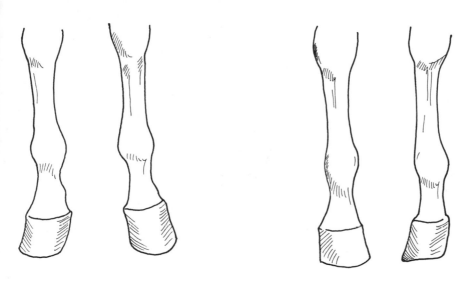

Toed out (left) and toed in (right). Selective trimming of the feet and specialised shoeing by a good farrier can often work wonders to help correct these tendencies.

After the first month it is important that the foal's feet should be checked regularly. The slightest amount of uneven growth in a young foot can cause uneven growth in the limb above, which will cause problems later when the animal is brought in to work. The feet must be trimmed by a qualified farrier. Obviously some feet grow quicker than others and without regular attention they will crack, split or even break off in large pieces. It takes nine months to a year (for an adult and half this time for foals) for the top of the hoof to grow out to the bottom, so any damage takes a long time to rectify. This is why it is so important to start checking the foal's feet early in its life so that any abnormalities, such as front feet turning in or out, upright heels or clubby feet, can be corrected before it is too late.

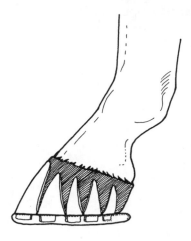

Many foot problems, particularly in adult horses with brittle hooves, can be helped by the use of plastic stick-on shoes.

The foot of the horse is a very complex structure, and the following basic description may help the reader to understand the function of the various parts. The wall of the hoof, which covers the outside of the foot, is made of a strong hard substance called the *horn*. This grows from the coronary band at the top of the hoof. The horn is the protective covering and is insensitive, unlike most of the foot which is sensitised by the nervous system. The *sole* of the foot also acts as a protection for the sensitive laminae and the pedal bone. The sole of the foot has no sensation of its own but it does bruise easily, especially in the case of Thoroughbreds. Some horses tend to be thinner-soled than others. Situated in the middle of the sole is a thick wedge-shaped cushion, the *frog*, which is

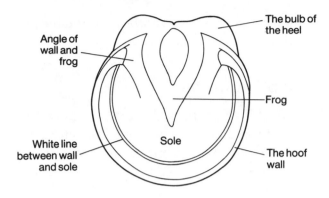

Angle of wall and frog

The bulb of the heel

Frog

White line between wall and sole

Sole

The hoof wall

The sole of the foot.

fitted point foremost into the angles of the heel. Its job is to absorb concussion, and so it does not bruise so easily as the sole.

Buried in the centre of the foot are the small bones, which form the last joint of the leg. These are the *pedal bone*, the *second phalanx* or *short pastern* and the *navicular bone* or *coffin bone*. Very strong ligaments pass from bone to bone holding them firmly in position, yet permitting all the necessary movement. The tendons run down from the muscles in the leg above, over the navicular bone and onto the pedal bone.

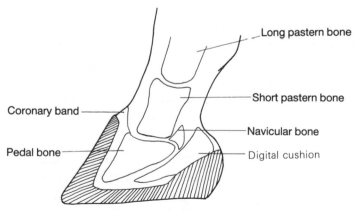

Long pastern bone

Short pastern bone

Coronary band

Navicular bone

Pedal bone

Digital cushion

The bones of the foot (cross-section).

125

The junction between the wall of the hoof and the pedal bone is made by the sensitive *laminae*.

Three to Six Months

At the age of five months the foal is ready to start its vaccination programme against equine influenza. A full outline of the vaccination programme and the relevant intervals between each injection will be found in Chapter 11, Injuries and Diseases.

It is desirable to wean the foal no later than six months after its birth. The foal is fully independent by this stage and is drawing on the mare unnecessarily when it suckles. If she is in foal again it is better that this extra drain on her resources is removed sooner rather than later.

Weaning methods have changed considerably over the last few years and are consequently less stressful for the foal. Years ago the weaning procedure was to separate mare and foal by putting them in two boxes as far away from one another as possible, so that they were out of each other's earshot. The foal would have been kept in its box for at least four or five days, which was in itself a shock. Inevitably there were accidents caused by frustration and loneliness and often the foal would go off its feed. Stable vices were often learned during this stressful stage.

However, today the whole process is much less problematic. The mares and foals are left out in the paddocks day and night during the whole of the summer. In this way the group get to know each other and they settle much better. In many ways they are living a life not too dissimilar to that of a herd in its natural state. It is preferable for weaning purposes to have the foals of the same age group together. By the time they are four to five months old they have already become more independent and will wander away from their dams to play together.

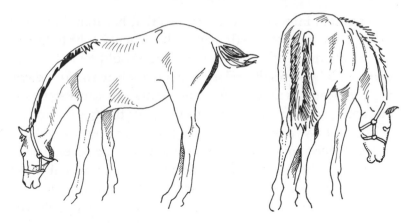

When foals are old enough to wander away from their dams to graze or play together they will be ready for weaning.

When they begin to do this it is an indication that the foals are ready to wean.

Once the decision has been made to wean the foals, the normal procedure is to take the mare with the oldest foal in the group out of the paddock first, leaving the foal with the others for company. It helps if the rest of the mares and foals can be kept well away from the gate while the weaned mare goes through it, and if possible it is best to hold the foal until the dam is well out of sight and hearing range. Of course the foal will be upset for a time but as the other animals settle and graze again the foal will soon follow suit. This process is carried out regularly until after a week or two the last mare is taken away.

If there is only one mare and foal then a companion is needed at weaning time. The companion will have been turned out with them both for quite a while before weaning and the foal will soon settle down again with it after the dam has been taken out. The subject of a companion has already been covered in Chapter 6.

The mare should be put in a stable out of calling or hearing range of the foal. She will obviously be upset for a day or two but it is important to do this so that her milk flow will dry up. She will start to dry up within twenty-four to thirty-six hours and in order to help her she should be fed a bran mash with Epsom salts in it once a day for three or four days. She can be fed as much hay as she wants. She can also be led out daily, so long as it is out of range of the foal.

The first day after weaning the bag is very large and hard to the touch. Sometimes it may be advisable to express a little milk from each teat but normally the mare will have run milk during the night which can be seen on her hind legs. This is all part of the process of drying up. By the second day of weaning the bag should already have reduced slightly in size. A small amount of wax from the teat can be rubbed on to the udder to stop it chafing while it is so swollen. Observation should be kept on the mare's milk bag for at least a fortnight, as there is still a real danger of an infection such as mastitis. Mastitis is an acute swelling of the bag and if it is not treated by a veterinary surgeon an abscess can form, which could cause problems the next time the mare has a foal to feed.

Mares and foals should be handled as much as possible

The more the foal is handled the better; here a foal is learning to lead quietly alongside its mother.

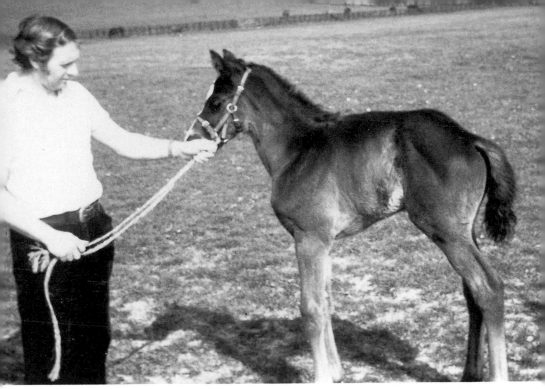

Foal abnormalities. (*Above*) This foal was born with fused vertebrae and cannot canter. (*Below*) This foal was born with a twisted face and very weak hind legs.

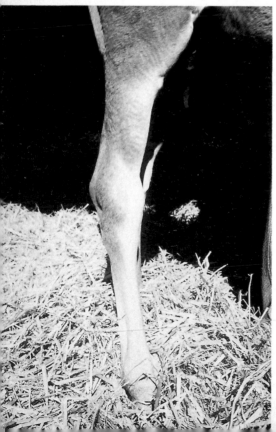

Foal abnormalities (*Above*) Foal over at the knee and (*Left*) joint ill of the hock.

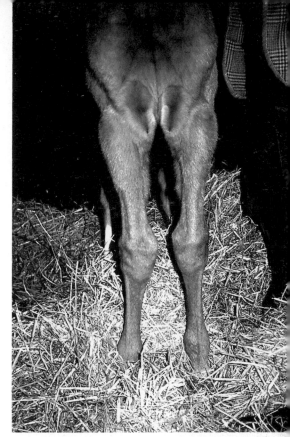

Foal abnormalities. (*Right*) Foal
with offset knees. (*Below*) Parrot
mouth in an older horse.

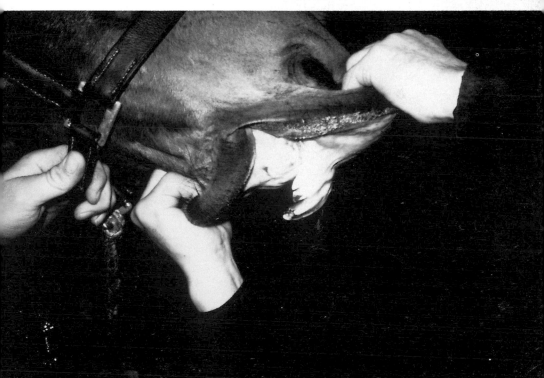

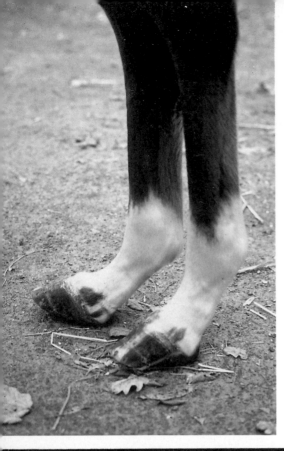

(*Left*) Foal with hyper extension of distal joints. (*Below*) The same animal six months later after corrective shoeing.

both before and after weaning, either by bringing them in to feed or by spending time with them when feeding them out in the field. This entails trying to persuade the foal to take a little food from the hand. It will soon respond to this and with a little coaxing and patience will come to hand quickly. It is also a good idea to ensure that the foal is good to lead at this stage as this will help quite considerably come winter time.

After Six Months

Some people keep their youngstock in covered yards all the time in winter, especially when the paddocks have become too wet. In any case foals should be brought in every night from October until the spring. Time should be taken to begin to brush them over and to pick their feet out, which will help to make the farrier's job easier, and they must also start to learn to stand tied up in the stable. The more time spent with foals the more readily they respond to new demands, and this helps particularly at the yearling stage.

Foals are like children and can be very temperamental, some more so than others; and so a firm hand is sometimes needed for the more irritable ones. Kindness must always be shown as well. Time and patience are needed to master them while they are still at the foal stage. Ill-treatment of bad-tempered and precocious foals will only serve to aggravate them and make them more apprehensive every time they have to be caught. It takes weeks for the foal to forget any ill-treatment sustained and sometimes they do not ever forget. A contented foal will come to hand as soon as the attendant enters the stable and every time this happens a pat and a few words of encouragement will go a long way towards increasing the foal's confidence.

By the time they are ten months old – the end of November or the beginning of December for the majority of Thoroughbreds – the foals are coming to hand easily and it is possible to go on to the next stage of their education if they seem ready for it. This stage involves starting to put a bit into the foal's mouth. Obviously for breeds other than the Thoroughbred which are not going to be broken and ridden as two-year-olds, it is not necessary to do this at this stage of the youngster's life. However, if you find that by this age the foals are becoming boisterous and hard to handle, to bit them now will help.

Nylon foal bit.

A foal bit is very light, with a straight mouthpiece made of nylon, and is attached to the D-rings of the headcollar by two connecting straps. Again, as at every stage of the foal's education, time and patience are needed and it is much easier if there are two attendants, one to hold the foal and the other to put the bit in. First of all let the foal look at the bit and smell it. Then, holding the bit between the forefinger and thumb, gently put the bit to the lips of the foal while opening the mouth with the other hand. As the foal opens its mouth gently slide the bit in and then buckle each side of the bit to the headcollar. Let the foal loose in the stable for a short period, so that it can feel the bit and get accustomed to it.

If this procedure is carried out two or three times a week the foal will soon accept the bit. However, the bit must *never* be forced into the mouth and if the foal is very reluctant to take it, try putting a little honey on the bar of the bit in order to make it more enticing to the foal. Once the bit is accepted continue to bit the foal until it reaches the yearling stage.

10

Handling a Yearling

All registered Thoroughbred foals become yearlings on 1 January, even though some of them may have been born as late as June. This is the reason for trying to have early foalings, as it gives the youngsters a little bit of a head start against those that were foaled later when they start to race as two-year-olds. An early foaling is not so important in breeds which are not required to start their working life until later than the Thoroughbred racehorse.

At the end of the previous chapter I described the process of bitting a foal. This can now be carried on to the next stage and the bit can be attached to a light bridle rather than to the headcollar.

As a general rule, breeds other than the Thoroughbred are not bitted so early, and if you are breeding late-maturing competition horses they will not be backed until they are three to four years old. However, the principles of regular handling still apply, and the more the yearling is accustomed to being handled the fewer the problems you are likely to encounter when the time comes to back the horse later in life. Feet should be picked up daily so that this becomes second nature to the horse; this also assists the blacksmith when he comes to rasp them. Tying up is also essential but must be done with care. It is advisable to do this for no more than a few minutes at a time, and always with someone in attendance in case the youngster should panic. All yearlings should be taught to lead quietly. This is

131

especially important for show stock: when showing young-sters in the ring they normally wear a showing headcollar with a lead rein.

When introducing the Thoroughbred yearling to the bit and bridle, to begin with the head piece should be un-buckled at the side of the animal's head as if the bridle were a headcollar, to which the animal will have been accustomed all its life. The bit should be put in its mouth and the king piece gently and quietly put over its neck and brought up behind the ears so that the strap can be buckled up again, and the yearling will be wearing a bridle for the first time. Again it cannot be stressed enough that great care must be taken at this stage as some youngsters are by nature a bit shy about the head. Once it is possible to put the bridle on without first unbuckling the king piece it is time to change bits.

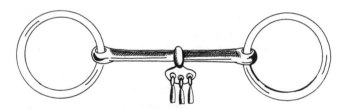

Mouthing bit with keys.

The new bit to use is either a stainless steel plain snaffle or a mouthing bit with three keys hanging from its centre. This is a much larger bit both in size and shape and the yearling may be a little apprehensive about accepting it at first. If the bit is immersed in warm water before being put in the yearling's mouth, it will stop the youngster being shocked by the feel of the cold steel. Again the bit can be left in the mouth for about an hour, so that the youngster gets into the habit of playing with the keys with its tongue and so learns to mouth correctly.

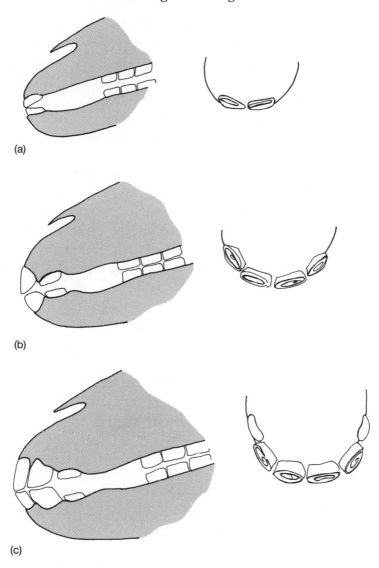

(a)

(b)

(c)

(a) *At birth the foal has two central incisors and three premolars or cheek teeth emerging.*
(b) *At around six weeks the lateral incisors start to appear on either side of the central ones.*
(c) *By the time the youngster is nine months old the corner incisors will also be through the gums.*

Never be in a hurry when introducing a new bit to a yearling as it can throw its head up at any stage of bitting and if the bit is not quite in the mouth, the animal could be hit in the teeth or face or eye, which will only make it more apprehensive the next time it was bitted.

Before the youngster is led out in hand on a bit it is vitally important that its teeth are checked by a veterinary surgeon or a horse dentist for any sharp edges or irregularities. It is unlikely that the teeth will need rasping at this stage, but if they do this procedure should always be carried out professionally as explained in Chapter 3. The horse's mouth has six incisors in each jaw. These are the central, lateral and corner teeth, and there are two of each. The foal when born has two central incisor teeth, or at least these will just be erupting from the jaw. At about six weeks of age the lateral teeth appear and at eight months the corner incisors are through the gums. These teeth are all temporary and it takes about five years for the temporary teeth to be replaced by the permanent ones. The horse also has six molars on each side of both the upper and lower jaws. The front three molars are present at birth or shortly afterwards. These teeth do not grow to a certain length and then stop growing; instead, they continue to grow right through to old age. They get worn down by the continual grinding of the teeth while feeding, but animals fed on hard feed tend to wear the teeth unevenly and the resulting sharp edges can cause discomfort and even serious sores in the animal's mouth. A regular dental check will prevent the mouth from reaching this painful state.

Once the yearling has fully accepted the bit it is time to walk it out using the bit to control it. Always bear in mind that the bit can be very brutal to a soft mouth. Care must be taken that the bit is neither too high nor too low in the mouth. It should be high enough so that the corners of the mouth pucker slightly, but not too much, and the king piece should

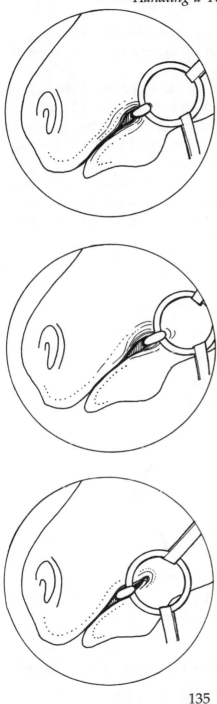

It is important that the bit is correctly fitted in the yearling's sensitive mouth. It should be just high enough to pucker the corners of the mouth a little (top). It should not be too high (centre) nor too low (bottom).

be buckled tightly enough so that the bit does not hang loosely in the mouth and bang against the teeth when the animal moves its head.

A connecting strap should be attached to the cheek rings of the bit underneath the jaw and there should be a central ring on the strap to which a lunge line can be clipped. To begin with, however, it is a good idea to attach the hand lunge to the nearside of the headcollar, while putting the forefinger through the ring on the jaw strap and gently putting pressure on the bit. This will accustom the yearling to pressure on the bit without having to lead him on it

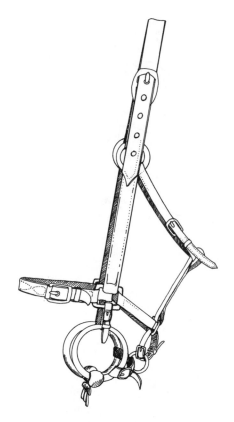

A yearling headcollar complete with breaking bit and attachments.

immediately. After a few days the lunge line can be transferred to the central ring on the jaw strap, but be careful not to pull too hard on the lunge, otherwise the yearling could rear up and come over backwards. It is advisable to attach a very small connecting strap from the back 'D' of the headcollar to the central ring of the jaw strap, as this can prevent the jaw strap from being pulled down severely into the animal's mouth in the event of it getting excited or frightened. The attendant should talk to the youngster as much as possible without raising the

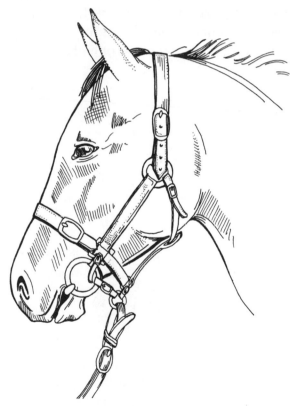

Walking the yearling on the bit. A connecting strap should be attached to the rings of the bit underneath the jaw and there should be a central ring on the strap to which a lunge line can be clipped.

voice. This will help to increase its confidence, as will the occasional pat down the shoulder.

As the walking progresses the attendant should walk as briskly as possible, so that the animal really starts to extend itself in order to keep up. Walking at a good pace with the yearling helps to promote muscle and if this is carried out for about six weeks it will prove most beneficial to the animal at the next stage of its education, whether it is to be broken to saddle, prepared for the sales or the show ring or, if a Thoroughbred, made ready to go into training. It is preferable to walk in the open air rather than in a covered school if possible, as the key to all lessons is to avoid monotony. However, the quiet of the surroundings is the most important factor, especially in the case of highly bred and excitable

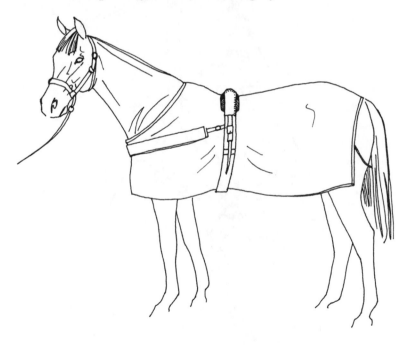

It is wise to accustom the yearling to the feel of wearing a rug. If a roller is used to hold the rug in place it must not be too tight. A breast strap can be a good idea to ensure that the roller does not slip back.

colts and fillies. Excitement and nervousness take far more out of a yearling than any amount of quiet work.

It is worth mentioning rugging-up at this stage. Obviously youngsters have to be acclimatised to this just like any other idea. At first put a light summer sheet on for short periods every day. If a leather roller is used to keep the sheet in place, make sure that it is well oiled and do not over-tighten it, otherwise the animal may fight to get rid of it, quite apart from the danger of galling the soft skin. A breast strap is a good idea as it helps to stop the roller slipping back. Many people do not bother with rugs at this time, but they are certainly helpful to keep the coat in good condition when showing youngsters in hand, and if the yearling is to go into training it will be well accustomed to the feel of a rug before the onslaught of winter and the heavier rugs.

As I have said many times before, the more young stock are handled the fewer problems arise later. In the case of a yearling bred for flat racing it will be made to enter the starting stalls as an early two-year-old. This can be a most unnerving experience and if not handled correctly can cause all sorts of complications, such as a horse refusing to go into the stalls; rearing up in the stalls and unseating the rider, which can be extremely dangerous; or bolting out of them when they are opened, which can cost the animal the race.

It is therefore a good idea to build mock starting stalls, so that the youngster is well accustomed to them before being confronted by the real thing. These do not need to be of elaborate design so long as they are made from strong wood and wire mesh. Two or three stalls side by side is the best arrangement. Each stall should be 7ft 6in (2.3m) long, 3ft (.9m) wide and 7ft 6in (2.3m) high. They should be boarded from the ground up to a height of 3ft 8in (1.1m) and then the wire mesh should be used for the top section, as can be seen in the photograph. If mock starting stalls are available it is a good idea to start walking the foals through them and then halt them for a while before leading them out. By the time they are yearlings they will have no fear of the stalls and the procedure will be second nature to them.

Colts are usually castrated during the yearling stage, but obviously this decision does depend on the future plans for the youngster. Some colts become sexually mature during the yearling stage and are more advanced than others, and this can create a problem on the stud or in the stable. They may run up and down the fence, calling to the others and never really settle down. If the colt is a Thoroughbred and bred for racing it is possible to send him into training early, as the work often helps to settle them, but others continue to have the same behaviour pattern throughout their two- and three-year-old careers. They do not learn to concentrate and become more and more temperamental so that in these cases the best option is to castrate them.

If a colt is not particularly well-bred, has a conformation fault or is possibly the only colt in the stable, then it is probably a sensible decision to have him castrated. Some animals do actually benefit physically from the operation. This is especially true in cases where the colt is becoming over-topped for his limbs, although it can also work conversely and a yearling which is a poor doer can rapidly put on weight after castration.

During the early life of a colt the testicles move downwards gradually through the inguinal canal until they reach the scrotum, which they then fill. After this the scrotum will be visible behind the colt's hind legs. If it is visible and the testicles can be easily felt then they are ready to be removed without any particular difficulty and the colt will only require a general anaesthetic. However, in some cases only one testicle may have dropped, even in a colt as old as eighteen months, in which case the colt is known as a 'rig'. It is then necessary for the animal to have a major operation so that the hidden testicle can be found and removed. Whichever method is used the recovery time from the operation seems to be remarkably quick, and as long as the animal continues to eat there is no reason to expect any complications.

11

Injuries and Diseases

A thorough knowledge of stable and stud management can help to prevent injury and illness, but however diligent one is there will always be accidents and outbreaks of disease. This chapter gives a simple description of the ailments you will come across when breeding horses and a brief explanation of the relevant treatments.

The first indication that a mare or youngster is not well is noticed from its overall demeanour. A healthy animal will look around and take notice when it is led out of its box, and when made to walk will take lengthy strides with a certain amount of awareness about its head; the eyes will be wide open and the ears pricking to and fro. The coat of the animal should look shiny and the skin should be loose and supple.

However, if the animal is not well it will walk with its head bowed, the eyes dull, ears slightly back; and the coat may have lost its sheen and be standing up or 'staring' instead of laying flat. When the skin is felt it is very tight to the muscles as if dehydrated. The membrane of the mouth and eyes is a deep red, as opposed to a pink colour in a healthy animal. At this stage the temperature of the animal should be taken. This is done by inserting the thermometer into the anus, but make sure that the mercury in the thermometer has been shaken down below the normal temperature before doing so.

In a healthy horse

THE PULSE is about 40 beats per minute.
THE RESPIRATION RATE is about 15 times per
   minute.
THE NORMAL TEMPERATURE is 100°F (37.8°C).

Nursing a sick mare or youngster involves attention to detail, no matter how minor. This is conducive to the patient's general comfort. The ventilation in the box is one of the main points to be remembered. There must be plenty of fresh air, but no draughts, as fully explained in Chapter 2. Horses do not need to be kept in a warm atmosphere, but they will fare much better if extremes of temperature are avoided. However, a very young foal may require a warm box, especially if it was born weak or if the weather conditions are very cold and damp. Rugs should be sufficient for warmth but not heavy. There are very light and thermally efficient rugs made specially for sick foals and yearlings which can be bought from the local saddlers. Bandages should be applied to the legs from below the knee to the coronet to keep the extremities warm, although as previously advised in Chapter 8 care should be taken not to bandage a foal (or any horse, for that matter) too tightly, or the bandages will impede the circulation.

Foals in particular must be fed little and often. Mares and yearlings, if sick, should be offered as many changes of food as possible, especially different varieties of green food. Water must be constantly within reach and changed frequently. Cooked oats or barley with well-cooked linseed are a good idea, not only because they are tempting but also because when mixed in a mash they help to keep the bowels open.

Wounds

These can be divided into five types.

Clean-cut wounds, which are caused by a sharp-edged object, are simply a division of the skin, and sometimes the under-lying muscle, without any loss of substance; but they do bleed freely. When the bleeding is stopped the two cut surfaces, not having been bruised or torn, will come to-gether again quickly, as long as the wound is kept clean. If it is a particularly long or deep cut then it may require stitching.

The fastest way to stop bleeding is to apply pressure. This can be achieved either by placing a pad on the wound and bandaging over it firmly or in severe cases by applying a tourniquet. The tourniquet should be put on the leg above the wound and must be tight enough to stop the bleeding, but it should only be used for half an hour at a time, or the small tissues will die from lack of blood and gangrene could set in to the wound. If the wound is on the chest a pressure pad must be used. Bleeding stops because the blood has clotted. Once this has happened the mouth of the wound can be dressed with an antiseptic powder. Once the wound has finally dried up and there is no more discharge, try to avoid getting it wet again.

Bleeding may be from an artery, a vein or from both. The blood from an artery is bright scarlet and spurts out in jerky jets, each successive jerk corresponding to the beat of the heart. The flow from a vein is much steadier and the blood is a darker red colour. Mixed bleeding is most commonly seen from ordinary wounds and comes from the small vessels which are so numerous all over the body.

There are eight gallons (approximately thirty-seven litres) of blood in a horse. The blood accounts for six-and-a-half per cent of the horse's body weight, and sixty per cent of the blood is made up of plasma. The white blood cells are most important in fighting infection, and it has been found that at times of excitement the red blood cell count increases quite markedly.

Minor injuries are often the result of yearlings galloping about and knocking themselves or bruising one another in play.

Torn wounds, which are caused by protruding objects such as barbed wire or nails, do not bleed freely or heal as quickly as clean-cut wounds. Often parts of the torn flesh may die and the dead pieces have to be cut away before healing can occur. Such wounds are treated in the same way as clean cuts, but they always require stitching and a tetanus injection will probably have to be given.

Bruised wounds are the most difficult to treat. They are often caused by kicks or knocks. Yearling colts are particularly prone to them, as they do play so boisterously. It is not only the wound that needs healing but also the bruising that surrounds it. These wounds should not be overlooked just because they do not appear serious at the time, for within a few hours the swelling can worsen considerably and the

145

wound be enlarged as a result. The healing time will have been increased by neglect. Again, as in the case of the torn wounds, there is often a loss of skin around the wound, which does not bleed very much, and the proud flesh may have to be cut away later. An Animalintex poultice will be found very useful for counteracting the swelling.

Puncture wounds are found mostly in the feet of the animal. They are usually caused by treading on nails or sharp slivers of flint or other stone or by thorns piercing the skin or even the wall of the hoof. These punctures can be very difficult to treat because the small opening in the skin or hoof closes immediately, sealing in the dirt, if the seat of the problem is not discovered earlier. It is not always possible to find the injury before this has occurred. If the inflammation is on the skin, a hot poultice will help to draw the infected matter to the surface. If the infection occurs in the foot, a poultice on the sole will help to draw it out. Sometimes, however, a farrier may have to be called to find the place which is causing the heat and inflammation and to enlarge the opening in order to thoroughly clean the wound under-neath. Once this is done a poultice should be applied; preferably an Animalintex as this is easy to use and can be held in place with an elastic adhesive bandage.

It is better to avoid using a poultice boot on a youngster, especially if the treatment is to be lengthy. The youngster will favour the uninjured leg in any case but the boot will exaggerate this problem and the unbalanced weight distri-bution will damage the growing feet, causing them to contract and spread respectively. A kaolin poultice can be very useful in cases of bruising, but it has a doughy consistency which can block the drainage of the pus from the foot. If the puncture is too deep to treat, the pus may be forced up through the foot and erupt at the first softer place it reaches, namely the coronary band.

Joint wounds should never be fermented or poulticed. Around the joint there is an airtight sac, which contains joint fluid. This fluid lubricates the surface of the joint. If this sac is punctured, an open joint wound is the result. The escaping joint fluid will be seen running from the wound and clotting in a thick yellowish mass below it. A poultice would only cause more joint fluid to be extracted, and this must be avoided. The flow of joint fluid must be stemmed as soon as possible, by running a constant stream of cold water over the wound. Once the flow has stopped the wound can be dressed, but if there is any doubt in your mind it is advisable to call the veterinary surgeon.

Cleanliness is the key to successful treatment of all wounds: cleanliness of the dressing and of the dresser. Natural substances such as salt or honey are very effective for healing. Salt in a warm water solution can be used for rinsing the wound and honey can be used in the dressing. Hydrogen peroxide is helpful if used after rinsing the wound, especially with puncture wounds in regions where the natural stone is very acidic because the acid does taint the wound. Pevidine is a very good antiseptic wash and sulphonamide powder can be used instead of honey. When wounded, the animal's body will produce extra white blood cells to combat the bacteria. The white cells that die while killing the bacteria are expelled from the wound in the form of pus.

Fractures

These are frequent among foals and are usually caused by kicks or by the youngsters running into things whilst galloping after their dams. The most common sites for fractures are the jaw, the spine, the pelvis and the limbs. If the bone is not seriously damaged the swelling will go down over the course of a few days, but if it is cracked and badly bruised there is usually a persistent flat swelling, which is hard to the touch, accompanied by a marked lameness. Fractures of the sesamoid bones in foals sometimes happen in the first month and these may not be noticed until they show up more as the foal grows. The sesamoid bones are situated behind the fetlock joint. Any suspected fractures should be X-rayed.

Concussion

Like fractures, concussion is usually caused by kicks or by running into things such as post and rail fencing, but it can also happen if the foal bumps its head badly in the box. The main symptom is that the foal behaves as if it was drunk. The best treatment is to ensure that the foal is kept warm and quiet and that it gets plenty of rest. It is most important that it does not eat, since it is only partly conscious and could choke on any food it is given.

Leg and Foot Injuries

The best pace for diagnosing lameness is a slow trot. The animal should be trotted away from and back towards the person examining it, without it being excited. When a horse is lame, it takes as much weight as possible off the injured or painful limb and places it on to the opposite limb. The extra weight placed on to the sound side makes the horse's action seem uneven. If the horse is lame on a foreleg, then it will be seen to bob its head when trotting towards you every time the sound foot comes to the ground. If it is lame behind, you will see that the hock of the sound leg will rise higher and dip lower than the lame one when the horse is trotted away from you.

Filling of the legs is seen most often in older brood mares because of poor circulation. Fluid builds up in the hind legs, which fill considerably, but as soon as the mare is exercised the filling subsides.

Lymphangitis is a more serious sequel. This occurs in the hind leg when a cut becomes infected and the infection spreads up the lymphatic vessels causing a hot, painful swelling. This condition must be treated with a course of antibiotics and diuretics if necessary.

Epiphysitis is a condition that foals may suffer from as they are growing. It involves the swelling of the fetlock growth plates and can appear as early as six to eight weeks old. The foal may go lame, with upright pasterns which may go bandy. The fetlock joint will be very painful when touched. Epiphysitis affects yearlings in much the same way but at this stage it involves the growth plates just above the knee or hock rather than the fetlock. Very painful swelling is evident, with upright limb or bandy foreleg. Veterinary help should be sought as this condition in either foals or yearlings may necessitate box rest and a change of diet. The help of a farrier might also be advisable.

Splints. If a youngster gallops on hard ground too much in the summer it may throw a splint. This means that the ligament which attaches the splint bone is torn. Occasionally there is some initial lameness and soft swelling. This soft swelling gradually turns into a bony enlargement and in most cases causes no further problems. Splints are most commonly found on the inside of the foreleg. Obviously if the youngster is lame it should be given box rest and have the leg poulticed until it recovers; otherwise there is little action that can be taken.

149

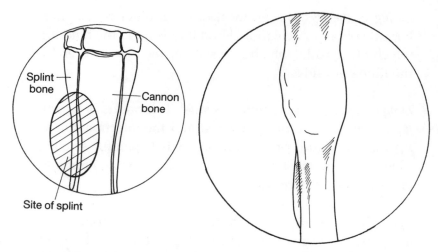

Splints are most commonly found on the inside of the foreleg.

Grass cracks also appear in dry weather if the horse's feet have not been trimmed regularly. The crack starts at the ground and then splits up the hoof. The farrier should be able to rectify this problem.

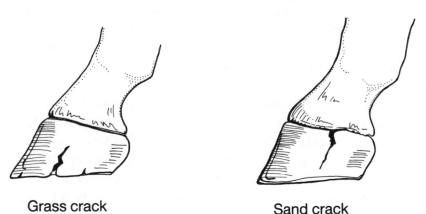

Grass crack   **Sand crack**

Sand cracks are the opposite. The crack starts at the top of the hoof and extends downwards. Usually caused by an injury to the coronary band, these cracks can result in lameness from the pain experienced if the split closes on the sensitive

150

parts underneath and in extreme cases may even cause bleeding. The farrier should be called as soon as possible.

Cracked heels are especially common on animals with white hair around the pastern and fetlock joint. They occur more often in winter when the climatic conditions encourage them as the grass does not dry out and the skin at the back of the pastern becomes chapped, sore and hot. The best treatment is to keep the heels clean and dry until a zinc-based ointment has cleared the problem. If the animals must be turned out in muddy conditions, it is advisable to cover the white parts with a protective smear of Vaseline or udder cream to prevent cracked heels from forming.

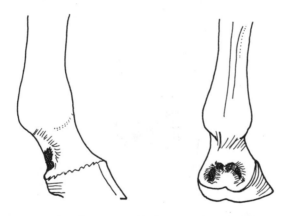

Cracked heels

Laminitis, otherwise known as fever in the feet, is an inflammation of the laminae, which are the fleshy leaves beneath the wall of the hoof and which cover the pedal bone. The symptoms are heat and pain in both forefeet. The horse is usually in so much pain that it is unwilling to pick up either front foot and if it is made to walk it will try to walk on its heels. In severe cases laminitis is recognised by the flat sole and is caused by the pedal bone dropping down and pushing the sole outwards. Ponies are very prone to this condition, especially if they eat too much rich grass. However, incorrect feeding, shock and undue stress can also bring on these symptoms. A mare who retains a portion of the afterbirth may suffer from laminitis, and a fall in pH levels is associated with the onset of both laminitis and colic. The farrier's help is a must in the treatment of this illness, as the front shoes may have to be removed whilst the patient is given box rest, or alternatively he may have to fit special bar shoes to the front feet to help take the horse's weight off the dropped sole of the foot.

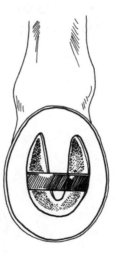

The farrier's help is a must in the treatment of laminitis. This horse has been shod with a bar to help raise the sole of the foot from the ground and a plastic stick-on shoe to minimise discomfort in feet which will be far too painful for a conventional shoe.

Thrush is caused by dirt and damp in a warm environment when the horse is standing in its stable for long periods. General neglect of the feet is mainly to blame. The treatment is to wash and clean the feet in salt water to remove the foul-smelling black discharge which is chiefly found in the angles of the frog. Flush the feet out with hydrogen peroxide and dress them with purple spray or Stockholm tar.

Blood Disorders

Nettle rash is a relatively harmless form of blood disorder which can appear very suddenly. Fluid is thrown out from the bloodstream, which causes soft lumps and bumps to form all over the body, and the eyes and nostrils to swell up. The animal's overall appearance can come as a shock when it is first seen, but the lumps and swellings can all disappear just as quickly as they arrived and after twenty-four hours there is nothing to be seen.

Colic

Colic is the name given to a series of symptoms which horses show when they suffer pains in the belly. The condition is non-contagious but potentially serious, and immediate veterinary attention should be sought. The pain may be due to a variety of causes but whatever the cause the symptoms exhibited are very similar. In the majority of cases colic is connected to food and feeding routines, for example unsuitable or unsuitably prepared food or a sudden change of diet. Other cases can be caused by worm impaction, gross sickness, twisted gut or bowel or, in the case of in-foal mares, by abortion.

In *spasmodic colic* the pain is not continuous, so that there are intervals of ease between the spasms during which the animal looks quite well until another spasm occurs. The horse is generally violent in its actions; it paws the ground, stamps and tries to kick at its belly; lies down, rolls, gets up and stretches itself as if trying to stale; looks around at its sides; sweats on the neck and, in severe cases, all over. The pulse is fast and the breathing hurried and distressed. The lining of the eye is bright red, but the temperature may remain normal. As the attack progresses the pains become more frequent and last longer, but when relief is given the symptoms disappear very quickly.

Another form of colic is caused by fermentation of the food in the bowels, which become distended by the resulting gases. The belly is enlarged and the pain is continuous but not as violent as in the case of spasmodic colic. The animal is uneasy and fidgety, scraping at the floor and attempting to lie down, but afraid to do so. The pulse will be fast but the temperature normal.

Both conditions are usually accompanied by severe constipation during the whole attack. Treatment by a veterinary surgeon is aimed at achieving two objectives: the first is the immediate relief of the pain and the second is to relax the animal. This is done with injections. If impaction still persists, direct tubing of the stomach with a solution of oil, salt and water is the answer. Opinion is divided about the practice of keeping the animal moving until the veterinary surgeon's arrival: it is difficult to say whether the walking achieves anything or whether it benefits the horse at all. As a footnote, it is hard to believe that the horse has a seventy-foot-long gut!

Tetanus

This is a harmful bacteria which is found in the ground. The bacteria find their way into any open wound and will quickly cause septicaemia, especially in foot wounds such as a punctured sole, but any wound which comes into contact with the soil can become infected. The symptoms are excitability coupled with restricted movement, and a fleshy membrane, the 'third eyelid', can be seen across the eye. The animal may well die, as treatment is prolonged, expensive and often unsuccessful. However, the disease can be immunised against with anti-tetanus injections and these are highly efficient. The tetanus booster can be administered at the same time as the flu vaccination once the course has been correctly started.

Humans are also at risk from the tetanus germ and anyone working with horses should be advised to make sure that they too have tetanus injections with a regular booster at intervals as recommended by a doctor.

Contagious Diseases

Coughs and colds are frequent visitors to mares, foals and yearlings and are caused by a virus. Foals seem to be particularly susceptible to them when they are weaned, probably because their resistance has been lowered by the stress they experience at this time. Sudden changes of temperature and exposure to draughts can also lower a horse's resistance to a cold virus.

The symptoms of a cold are a discharge from the nostrils, which is watery at first but in the course of a few days becomes greyish and thickens and then turns a yellowish colour; but it does not smell. The horse can run a high temperature of 104°F (40°C) or more and have swollen glands in the head and neck before eventually developing a cough. Treatment for the cold is based on common sense. Keep the horse warm and comfortable and if the nasal discharge becomes intense then the horse can be steamed with Friar's Balsam in much the same way that one would steam a human cold.

Equine influenza causes an initial fever after which the cough is really the only major symptom. The influenza virus causes the inflammation of the lining of the bronchioles, which in turn causes the coughing. A cough is a defence against material entering the lungs, but repeated coughing is a

155

warning of excessive irritation, as in the instance of equine flu, and if it is not relieved it can cause damage to the heart and lungs. Unfortunately foals are especially susceptible to equine influenza.

The patient should be nursed in much the same way as for a cold, but obviously there is no need for steaming. It is vital though that the horse's lungs are not put under any extra strain while fighting this infection, so youngsters must not be turned out to gallop.

The surest method of prevention is to have all stock immunised against the virus. Foals can be vaccinated from five months onwards. If the virus is then brought into the yard none of the horses will suffer severely from it, if at all. This is also why it is so important to keep competing animals away from breeding stock, as racehorses or competition horses may well pick up the cough on their travels to racecourses or shows, only to bring it back to an otherwise uninfected yard.

The vaccination programme under the Rules of Racing is as follows. Two injections for primary vaccination should be given not less than twenty-one days or more than ninety-two days apart. A booster injection must then be administered between 150 and 215 days after the second injection of the primary vaccination. Subsequent booster injections must be given within the next twelve months from that date, and so on thereafter. This programme satisfies most other competitive ruling bodies as well: if in doubt, owners of other competition stock should check with the governing body of their particular sport.

It is recommended that any horse which develops a cough whilst stabled should be given hay and bedding which do not contain dust and contaminants such as fungus spores, mildew, mould and pollen dust. Hay can be soaked in water and drained before feeding, as the irritant spores stick to the stems when wet, which renders them harmless. The feeding value of the hay is not affected by soaking. Alternatively it might be easier to feed a product like Horsehage. Horsehage consists of clover and molasses and is commonly given to animals which have a history of respiratory problems since it is free from dust and pollen and is high in protein. It should be fed in small quantities. Horsehage is available from any good feed merchant and is supplied in sealed plastic bags.

Some horses develop a cough as a sign of an allergic reaction to something in their environment. Wheat straw has always been used as a comfortable bedding for horses. However, it can contain the same contaminants as hay. In addition some of the modern chemical sprays used on the crops have been found to cause allergic reactions in horses. Obviously if a horse suffering from a cough is kept in a dusty atmosphere the cough will progressively worsen. So a change in bedding is suggested, either to paper or to clean wood shavings, to ensure that dust levels are not a respiratory hazard. Wood shavings, however, are not entirely dust-free, and paper must be kept as dry as possible.

If a horse develops a cough whilst out at grass and has no other symptoms, it would be preferable to leave the animal where it is rather than confine it in a dusty environment. Most of these coughs will disappear without treatment so long as dust is avoided. Nevertheless it might be advisable to administer another wormer as some worms, such as lung worms, cause coughs.

Strangles, like the cold, is common among youngstock when they are turned out together in large numbers after weaning. The condition is very contagious and has potentially serious complications. The early symptoms of strangles are very dirty noses running with yellowish or green discharge, a temperature of 103°F (39.4°C) or more and swollen glands. Eventually an abscess forms on the swollen glands at the angle of the jaw bones. Treatment consists of encouraging the abscess to come to a head, which is accomplished by hot fomentations. This usually takes a few days if treated twice daily. Once the abscess bursts the horse will start to recover: make sure the wound is kept clean by syringing out with a mild antiseptic wash. Again, careful sensible nursing and rest are the best treatment for this condition.

The *Equine Herpes Virus* can be divided into two types. EHV-type I is the respiratory strain and more severe symptoms can be caused by secondary bacterial infections. EHV-type II is the strain that can cause abortion in brood mares. *Equine Rhinopneumonitis* is one of the results of infection with the herpes virus, but it does not necessarily indicate an abortion. Both EHV types can be carried and transmitted by either sex and at any age, so it is vital that brood mares do not come into close contact with any horses which travel about the country for competition, whether racing, eventing, show-jumping or whatever.

At the beginning of a virus abortion infection the mare may well run a temperature, look dull and go off her food. There may not necessarily be any discharge from her nostrils, so it is quite possible for this stage to pass unnoticed. It is the discharge that carries the virus. Later on as in the case of strangles there is a swelling of the glands of the throat under the jaw and a cough develops. If a mare does abort without any prior warning, she must be isolated from other horses immediately. The aborted foetus and placenta should be put in a clean plastic bag and the veterinary surgeon notified. He will then send them to a veterinary laboratory to be examined and it may be a few days until the results are received. During that time the mare must remain isolated and the following precautions should be taken. If the mare was in a stable at the time of the abortion, all the bedding should be burnt. The stable must be steam-cleaned and disinfected, as must all the stable implements such as brooms, forks and buckets. If staff numbers allow, it is best to keep one person to attend to the infected mare to minimise the risk of further infection.

If more than one mare is infected then the mares must be divided into three groups: the infected, the suspected and the healthy. The suspected are the mares which have been in contact with the infected mare, even though she may not have been showing any symptoms at the time. They should be removed from the vicinity and kept well away from any healthy mares.

Sexually Transmitted Diseases

Contagious Equine Metritis is a potentially damaging infection which causes infertility and unless it is cleared up with a course of antibiotics the mare will be unable to conceive. Fortunately breeders and stud owners are rigorous in their efforts to prevent the disease. Stallions of most breeds are tested regularly for contagious equine metritis and all mares have to be tested and certified free of the disease before going to stud.

Klebsiella is another sexually transmitted infection which both mare and stallion owners must constantly guard against, and most stallion studs will expect any visiting mare to have been tested and certified free of this disease.

Equine Viral Arteritis is a disease which can be carried by stallions, even though they themselves do not show any symptoms. If passed on to the mare, however, it can cause serious illness and can cause abortions. EVA is extremely rare in this country, and stringent efforts are being made to ensure that it remains so. Most reputable studs are currently taking precautions to prevent any outbreak from occurring by testing their stallions regularly, and mare owners can expect the stallion to have a veterinary certificate stating that he has been blood tested negative before the start of the covering season.

Other Infections

Mastitis is an infection of the mammary glands, which will be hot, very hard and painful for the mare. If mastitis is present it is not possible to extract any milk from the infected teat. If not picked up on and treated with antibiotics, the infection may permanently affect the mare's milk production in the future. The necessary antibiotics are given by means of a syringe with a very fine nozzle, in place of a needle, which is inserted into the teat.

Haemolytic anaemia or yellow jaundice has been covered in some detail in Chapter 8. Antibodies can be carried by the mare with no apparent symptoms, but the antibodies which will be present in the mare can unfortunately pass the disease on to the foal in the colostrum which would normally protect it. If this happens, the foal will become very sleepy and its heart rate and breathing rate will increase dramatically. Its urine will be dark red in colour and the foal's upper lip will turn yellow. Veterinary attention is necessary.

If it is known that the mare is carrying haemolytic antibodies before the foal is born, the foal can be protected from the disease by preventing it from suckling for thirty-six hours. The foal must be fed by hand and the mare milked to remove the colostrum. An alternative source of colostrum must be found for the foal to replace the colostrum it has been unable to take from its dam, or if this is not available protection from infection must be supplied by the vet in the form of antibiotics.

The mare should be tested in future before she foals to check for the presence of the disease.

Essential First Aid

Every stud or stable should have a first aid cabinet which contains the following essential items:

Thermometer, antiseptic wash, wound powder, bandages, gamgee gauze, Animalintex, heel bug jelly, Vaseline, antiseptic spray for feet, cornucresine, eye ointment, cotton wool, liquid paraffin, baby's bottle with teat, surgical scissors, plastic bucket and sponge.

Appendix I

The following list contains the recommended quantities for seed mixtures for horse pastures. (Taken from *The Veterinary Record*, 23 August 1980.)

Main Pasture Grasses:
    Perennial ryegrass (prostrate)
      late heading variety
    e.g. S23. melle, perma, miltra,   Two of these for half
    petra, semperweide & endura   the mixture
    Creeping red fescue,   Two of these for a
    e.g. S59. reptans, etc.   quarter of the mixture

Essential additions:
    Crested dog tail   @ 1kg per acre
    Rough-stalked meadow grass
      on wet areas   @ 1kg per acre
    Smooth-stalked meadow grass
      on dry areas   @ 1kg per acre
Wild white clover   0.25kg per acre
Herb mixture to include:–
    Chicory (cichorium imlybus)   1kg per acre
    Plantain (piantago lanceotata)
    Dandelion (taraxacum officinate)
    Yarrow (achillea millefolium)
    Burnet (poterium sanguisorba)
    Sheep's parsley (petroselinum crispum)
Original additions:–
    Timothy S48   1–2kg per acre
    Cocksfoot (late heading type)   "
    Agrostis for turf only   "
    Tall fescue for special purposes   2–2½kg per acre

Clover should never be sown at more than half a pound per acre (0.05kg per hectare), and it must only be wild white clover; no other clover is satisfactory.

Appendix II

FEED TABLES

Every horse owner has his or her own ideas about feeding, and most breeders or stud-grooms will have established their own system, based on experience and adjusted according to the nutritional value of the available grazing. Some large studs nowadays employ a full-time professional nutritionist to analyse and advise on the horse's feed content.

The feed tables that follow are the result of my own experience and demonstrate the feeding regime for mares, foals and yearlings followed successfully for many years at Angmering Park Stud.

Ration for In-Foal Mares with Foal at Foot

	Feedstuff	Quantity	Bone Meal	Ground Limestone	Bean Meal	Cod Liver Oil
January February March	Crushed oats Chop Linseed mash* Hay	4–4½kg 10ltr 10kg	1ds	1ds	340g	60g
April	Crushed oats Chop Linseed mash Hay	4–4½kg 10ltr 5kg	1ds	1ds	340g	60g

| May
June
July
August
to
weaning | Crushed oats
Chop
(Turned out
night and
day) | 6kg | 1ds | 1ds | 340g | |

ds=dessert spoonful.

The mash consists of bran, linseed, boiled whole oats, honey, cod liver oil and one tablespoon of salt.

The appropriate feeding routine for barren and maiden mares is as follows:

April–November they should take all their nourishment from the paddocks, which should have iodised salt licks in them.

November–December: 2–2½kg of crushed oats with chaff and 3kg of hay daily and they will be brought in at night.

January–March: the hay intake should increase by up to 3–3½kg daily.

Ration for In-Foal Mares without Foal at Foot

	Feedstuff	Quantity	Bone Meal	Ground Limestone	Bean Meal	
January & February	Crushed oats Chop Linseed mash Hay	2–2½kg 8–10ltr 3kg	1ds	1ds	340g	
March	Crushed oats Chop Linseed mash Hay	2–2½kg 8ltr 5kg	1ds	1ds	340g	
April	Crushed oats Chop Linseed mash Hay	2–2½kg 8ltr 5kg	1ds	1ds	340g	

From June until the end of October all their nourishment should be exclusively from the paddocks.

November	Crushed oats Chop Hay	3½kg 5kg	1ds	230g		
December	Crushed oats Chop Linseed mash Hay	3½kg1ds 8–10ltr 8–10kg	1ds	230g		

The mash consists of bran, linseed, boiled whole oats, honey, cod liver oil and one tablespoon of salt.

Ration for Foals

Age	Feedstuff	Quantity	Ground Limestone	Bone Meal	Cod Liver Oil
From birth to 8 weeks	Mother's milk	Ad lib			
3rd month	Crushed oats Chop Linseed mash Hay	Up to 300g 1ltr ad lib			15g 15g
4th month	Crushed oats Chop Linseed mash Hay	Up to ½kg 1ltr ad lib			15g
5th month to weaning	Crushed oats Chop Linseed mash Paddock grazing	1½kg 5–6ltr day & night	1ds	1ds	20g
9th & 10th month	Crushed oats Chop Linseed mash Paddock grazing	2–2½kg 5–6ltr	1ds	1ds	30g
11th & 12th month	Crushed oats Chop Linseed mash Hay	2–3kg 6–8ltr ad lib	1ds	1ds	30g

The mash consists of bran, linseed, boiled whole oats, honey, cod liver oil and one tablespoon of salt.

Ration for Yearlings

	Feedstuff	Quantity	Ground Limestone	Bone Meal	Cod Liver Oil	Grnd Bean Meal
January & February	Crushed oats Chop Linseed mash Hay	5kg @ 8ltr 5kg	1tbsp	1ds	60g	100g
March	Crushed oats Chop Linseed mash Hay	5kg 8–10ltr 5kg	1tbsp	1ds	40g	100g
April	Crushed oats Chop Linseed mash Paddock grazing day & night	5kg 8–10ltr	1tbsp	1ds		230g
May	Crushed oats Chop Linseed mash Paddock grazing day & night	5½kg 8–10ltr	1tbsp	1ds		230g
June July August September	Crushed oats Chop Paddock grazing day & night	6kg	1tbsp	1ds		340g

The mash consists of bran, linseed, boiled whole oats, honey, cod liver oil and one tablespoon of salt.

Appendix III

Registration – (1) THOROUGHBREDS

CONDITIONS OF ENTRY

A   To be eligible to be registered in the General Stud Book a horse must be able either:
   (1)   to be traced down all lines of its pedigree to horses registered before 1 January 1980 in
      (a)   The General Stud Book, and/or
      (b)   Any of the following Stud Books:
         the American Stud Book, the French Stud Book, the Stud Books of Australia, New Zealand, South Africa, Japan, India, Argentina, Brazil, Chile, Colombia, Mexico, Panama, Peru, Uruguay, Venezuela, Belgium and Luxembourg, Denmark, Israel, Italy, Spain and Sweden (A-Register).
OR (2)   to prove satisfactorily eight recorded crosses consecutively with horses qualified as in category 1 above, including the cross of which it is the progeny, and to have satisfied the performance and approval conditions as set out for foals in section B (2) and (3) below.

For the purposes of the General Stud Book, horses in categories 1 and 2 above are designated 'Thoroughbred'.

B   In addition, a foal may be promoted from the Non-Thoroughbred Register published by Weatherbys and registered in the Appendix to the General Stud Book when the following conditions are all satisfied:
   (1)   The foal can prove satisfactorily eight recorded crosses consecutively with 'Thoroughbreds' (as designated above) including the cross of which it is the progeny.
   (2)   The foal can show in both the 'Thoroughbred' and Non-Thoroughbred sections of its pedigree, such performances in races open to 'Thoroughbreds' as to warrant its assimilation with 'Thoroughbreds'.

(3) The promotion is approved by the unanimous agreement of the International Stud Book Committee.

Notwithstanding the above Conditions the Proprietors of the General Stud Book reserve the overall right to decide what horses can at any time be admitted to, excluded, or removed from the General Stud Book and related publications.

Registration – (2) NON-THOROUGHBREDS

CONDITIONS OF ENTRY

BROODMARES

To be eligible for registration as a broodmare in this Register, a mare must be able to show:

1. That she has won a flat race, steeplechase or hurdle race under the Rules of Racing of any recognised Turf Authority or a Point-to-Point Steeplechase in Great Britain or Ireland, or
2. That she has bred such a winner, or
3. That she is closely related to such a winner, or
4. That she was herself registered as a foal in a previous volume of this Register, or
5. That she is registered as a broodmare in the General Stud Book, or
6. That being ineligible for registration in the General Stud Book, she is registered in the Stud Book of a Turf Authority outside Great Britain and Ireland, recognised by the Jockey Club and as defined in the Rules of Racing, or in certain circumstances, in the official Non-Thoroughbred Register of a Turf Authority outside Great Britain and Ireland, or
7. That though fulfilling none of the above conditions, she can show other reasonable cause for being considered eligible.

In addition to satisfying one of the above eligibility conditions, the mare must have a registered name under the Rules of Racing prior to registration as a broodmare.

STALLIONS

To be represented by produce in this Register, a stallion must:

1. Be registered as a stallion in the General Stud Book, or the Stud Book of a Turf Authority outside Great Britain and Ireland, recognised by the Jockey Club and as defined in the Rules of Racing, or
2. Be registered as a stallion in this Register by having been able to show:

Appendix III

a) That he has won a flat race, steeplechase or hurdle race under the Rules of Racing of any Turf Authority recognised by the Jockey Club and as defined in the Rules of Racing or a Point-to-Point steeplechase in Great Britain or Ireland, or

b) That he has already sired the winner of a race listed in 2.a) above, or

c) That he was himself registered as a foal in a previous volume of this Register, or

3. Though fulfilling none of the above conditions, have been accepted for stallion registration as 'pedigree unregistered' having passed an inspection for age, size, conformation, soundness, and freedom from disease, by an independent veterinary surgeon appointed by the Proprietors of the Register.

In addition to satisfying one of the above eligibility conditions, the horse must have a registered name under the Rules of Racing at the time of covering.

Notwithstanding the above Conditions the Proprietors of the Non-Thoroughbred Register reserve the overall right to decide what horses can at any time be admitted, excluded, or removed from the Register and related publications.

Reproduced by permission of Weatherbys Group Ltd.

H.I.S. REGISTERS

The National Light Horse Breeding Society (H.I.S.) is able to give owners the opportunity to have all horses properly identified, graded and registered. The identification and grading registers are an enlargement on the old Hunter Stud Book which they effectively replace. There are five types of registration (not including the Show Register); these are: The Identity Record, the Grade Two Mare Register, the Grade One Mare Register, the Filly Register and the Gelding Register.

The Identity Record
Providing their adult height exceeds 14.2 hh, ALL HORSES ARE ELIGIBLE FOR ENTRY ONTO THE SOCIETY'S IDENTITY RECORD, as there are no breeding restrictions on this basic register. All you need do is obtain an application form from the Society. The form provides for full details of the horse, a signed declaration from the owner and the completion of an identification chart by a qualified veterinary surgeon. On receipt of the completed application form and fee the owner will be issued with a Certificate of Identity. The Certificate will comprise a copy of the Identification Chart showing the markings of the horse, on reverse of which is entered details of its ownership etc. and the horse's identification number; there is also room for details of vaccinations to be recorded. This Certificate will stay with the horse throughout its life, being returned to the Society for amendment, change of ownership, etc. To be shown at affiliated shows, a horse must be entered on the Identity Record. Foals up to three months old may be entered at Shows but must subsequently be registered. Before they are four months old Unnamed Foals will be recorded under their dam and a naming fee charged at yearling stage.

The Mare Grades – Grade Two Mares
Entries must fulfil one of the following requirements:
  The Mare must first be identified by entry on the Identification Record.

After this she shall be eligible for registration if:
a)   Her sire is a Premium or Approved Stallion and her Dam is a Mare registered on the Grade Two or Grade One register (or the old Hunter Stud Book).
b)   Both her Sire and Dam's Sire are Premium or Approved Stallions.

170

Appendix III

c) She is awarded one of the Society's Premiums; or she wins or breeds the winner of a monetary prize in a class at a National, County or Affiliated Show.

d) She wins or breeds the winner of a monetary prize at an officially recognised B.H.S. Horse Trials or Dressage competition or an Affiliated B.S.J.A. Jumping competition.

e) She or her produce win races under the Rules of Racing or a Point to Point.

f) If she does not fulfil any of the above conditions, she can be inspected by one of the Society's Breeding Panel Judges and must provide a Veterinary Certificate stating that she is free from listed diseases and defects. To be eligible for inspection the Mare must be three years old or over and exceeding 14 hh 2in, a fee of £35.25 inc. V.A.T. is payable, in addition to the registration fee. This is to cover the Inspector's expenses and is not refundable in the event of the Mare not being accepted.

All Mares three years old or over must provide a Veterinary Certificate stating that they are free from listed diseases and defects, which are: Cataract, Bone Spavin, Stringhalt, Sidebone, Navicular Disease, Ringbone (high and low), and Shivering.

– Grade One Mares
Entry to the Grade One register is strictly by inspection only. Mares must apply for inspection and will be allocated to one of the Society's official Inspections, which will take place at centres throughout the country in the late summer and autumn of each year. Entries for Grade One Inspection will close annually on 1 August. To be eligible for inspection the Mare must be four years old or over and on the Society's Identity Record. Mares passed for Grade One will receive a Service Voucher valued at £100 to be used towards the service of the Mare by a Premium Stallion or Registered Stallion (Grade One). The Voucher may be used only once at any time during the three covering seasons following the date of the Inspection.

– Filly Registration
The Society has now introduced a new type of registration for Fillies.

The Filly Registration is for Fillies up to three years of age, adult height to exceed 14.2 hh. On reaching three years of age all registered Fillies will become eligible for entry to the Grade Two Mare Register upon receipt of a completed Grade Two

Registration Form and a Veterinary Certificate stating that they are free from listed diseases and defects. Failure to re-register a Filly as a Grade Two Mare at the age of three will result in the Filly Registration becoming void.

The Filly must first be identified by entry on the Identity Record, then a Filly shall be eligible for registration:

a) if her Sire is a Premium or Approved Stallion and her Dam is a Mare registered in the Grade One or Grade Two Register.
b) if both her Sire and Dam's Sire are Premium or Approved Stallions.
c) if she wins a monetary prize in a Class at a National, County or Affiliated Show.

– Geldings
A section of the Register is retained for the entry of geldings and this has always proved popular for owners wanting breeding papers for their horse.

New entries must fulfil one of the following requirements:

The gelding must first be identified by entry on to the Identity Record.

After this he will be eligible for registration if:

– Pedigree
(a) If its sire is a Premium or Approved Stallion and if its dam is a mare registered in Grade One or Grade Two.
(b) If both its sire and dam'sd sire are Premium or Approved Stallions.

– Prizes
(c) If it has won a monetary prize in Classes at a National, County or Affiliated Show.
(d) If it has won a monetary prize at an officially recognised B.H.S. Horse Trials, Dressage Competition or B.S.J.A. Affiliated Jumping Competition.
(e) If it has won or been placed in races under the Rules of Racing or Point-to-Point.

THE BENEFITS
This Identification and Grading programme is of benefit to the British Horse Breeding Industry as a whole and to individual breeders in particular.

The Identification scheme has made a great step forward in the identification of Equines. Any horse can now be adequately identified on application and issued with a set of papers which will prove its identity in cases of dispute or doubt.

More Mares are now eligible for the basic Stud Book registration of Grade Two; this means that there should be a corresponding rise in the number of progeny eligible for registration. The progeny of Grade One and Grade Two Mares by Premium or Approved Stallions are automatically eligible for registration. It is hoped that those horses in possession of authenticated papers will prove to be of higher value than horses of unknown or unproven breeding. If the registered blood-lines are followed we will be able to form and authenticate pedigrees which will be an aid to more selective and scientific breeding methods.

The Grade One register has enabled us to name some of the best Mares in the country as Grade One Mares. The standard is high and the Inspectors look for top class Mares capable of producing the performance horses of the future. Proven performance mares forward for Grade One will have their record taken into account. In years to come the prestige accorded to these Mares will be enormous and it is hoped that the results of selective breeding from these Mares will soon speak for themselves. Again the financial benefits when selling the progeny of Grade One Mares are proving to be great.

Reproduced by permission of The National Light Horse Breeding Society (H.I.S.)

Appendix IV

USEFUL ADDRESSES

The Arab Horse Society
Windsor House
Ramsbury
Nr Marlborough
Wilts
SN8 2PE

Tel: 01672 20782
Fax: 01672 20880

The British Bloodstock Agency
Queensberry House
High Street
Newmarket
Suffolk
CB8 9BD

Tel: 01638 665021
Fax: 01639 660283

The National Foaling Bank
Miss Johanna Varden, MBE
Meretown Stud
Newport
Shropshire
TF10 8BX

Tel: 01952 811234
Fax: 01952 811202

The National Light Horse Breeding Society (H.I.S.)
96 High Street
Edenbridge
Kent
TN8 5AR

Tel: 01732 866277
Fax: 01732 867464

The National Pony Society
Willingdon House
102 High Street
Alton
Hants
GU34 1EN

Tel: 01420 88333
Fax: 01420 80599

The National Stallion Association
School Farm
School Lane
Pickmere
Nr Knutsford
Cheshire
WA16 9JF

Tel: 01565 733222

The Thoroughbred Breeders Association
Stansted House
8 The Avenue
Newmarket
Suffolk
CB8 9AA

Tel: 01638 661321
Fax: 01638 665621

Weatherbys
Sanders Road
Wellingborough
Northants
NN8 4BX

Tel: 01933 440077
Fax: 01933 440807

Index

splints, 149
wounds, 144–7

jaundice, *see* haemolytic anaemia

Klebsiella, 87, 159

lameness, 148
laminitis, 45, 151
lime, 19, 20
loading ramp, 42

maiden mares, 88
  foaling, 105
  in-foal, 94
mastitis, 111, 128, 160
meconium, 104, 114

National Light Horse Breeding
  Society (HIS), 76
nervous disorders (of foals), 109
nutrition, 44–6
  carbohydrates, 45
  fibre, 48, 54
  minerals, 45–6
  vitamins, 46

old swards, 17

paddock maintenance, 18–29
  harrowing and rolling, 18–19
  topping, 21
  weeding, 21–2
placenta, 104–5
poisonous plants, 22, 24–7
possessive mares, 118
poultices, 146
premature foals, 110
presentation (of foal), 102
  problems of, 107
Pseudomonas, 87
pulse rate, 143
  of foal, 106

reproductive system (of mare),
  90–91, *90, 91*
respiration rate, 143
  of foal, 106

roller bars, 35
rupture, 114

scouring, 121–2
septicaemia, 116
soil content (and analysis), 19–21
stable vices, 77–9
stabling, 31–43
stallions
  compatibility with mare, 73–5
  handling, 80–6
stillborn foals, 108, 111
stitching (of vulva), 99
stud fees, 93

teasing, 86
teeth
  development of, 132–3
  rasping, 51
temperament, 77
temperature, 142, 143
  of foal, 106
tetanus, 154
tourniquet, 144
twins, 110

ultrasound scanning, 89, 110
umbilical cord, 103

vaccination, 87, 93, 122, 126, 156
viral abortion, 158–9

water supply, 29, 39, 47–8
'waxing up', 98
weaning, 126–8
Weatherbys, 93, 122
worm cycle, 22–3
worming, 23

yearlings
  bitting, 131–6
  handling, 131
  leading, 138
  rugging up, 139
  stalls training, 139
yellow jaundice, *see* haemolytic
  anaemia
Paddock and Pasture